AMERICAN
ENVIRONMENTALISM

AMERICAN SOCIAL MOVEMENTS

AMERICAN ENVIRONMENTALISM

Greg Barton, *Book Editor*

333.7

Daniel Leone, *President*

Bonnie Szumski, *Publisher*

Scott Barbour, *Managing Editor*

Stuart B. Miller, *Series Editor*

GREENHAVEN PRESS
SAN DIEGO, CALIFORNIA

THOMSON
—————✳—————™
GALE

Detroit • New York • San Diego • San Francisco
Boston • New Haven, Conn. • Waterville, Maine
London • Munich

Every effort has been made to trace the owners of copyrighted material. The articles in this volume may have been edited for content, length, and/or reading level. The titles have been changed to enhance the editorial purpose.

Library of Congress Cataloging-in-Publication Data

American environmentalism / Greg Barton, book editor.
    p. cm. — (American social movements)
   Includes bibliographical references and index.
   ISBN 0-7377-1043-8 (pbk. : alk. paper) —
ISBN 0-7377-1044-6 (lib. : alk. paper)
   1. Environmental history—United States—Juvenile literature.
2. United States—Environmental conservation and ethics—
Juvenile literature. 3. Environmental movement—United
States—Activism and preservation—Juvenile literature. I. Title.
II. Series.

Cover photo: © Hulton/Archive
Library of Congress, 32, 89, 174
The Rhode Island Historical Society, 25

Cover caption: Theodore Roosevelt and
John Muir on Glacier Point in Yosemite, Ca.

Printed in the USA

CONTENTS

CHAPTER 5 • NARRATIVES

FOREWORD

Historians Gary T. Marx and Douglas McAdam define a social movement as "organized efforts to promote or resist change in society that rely, at least in part, on noninstitutionalized forms of political action." Examining American social movements broadens and vitalizes the study of history by allowing students to observe the efforts of ordinary individuals and groups to oppose the established values of their era, often in unconventional ways. The civil rights movement of the twentieth century, for example, began as an effort to challenge legalized racial segregation and garner social and political rights for African Americans. Several grassroots organizations—groups of ordinary citizens committed to social activism—came together to organize boycotts, sit-ins, voter registration drives, and demonstrations to counteract racial discrimination. Initially, the movement faced massive opposition from white citizens, who had long been accustomed to the social standards that required the separation of the races in almost all areas of life. But the movement's consistent use of an innovative form of protest—nonviolent direct action—eventually aroused the public conscience, which in turn paved the way for major legislative victories such as the Civil Rights Act of 1964 and the Voting Rights Act of 1965. Examining the civil rights movement reveals how ordinary people can use nonstandard political strategies to change society.

Investigating the style, tactics, personalities, and ideologies of American social movements also encourages students to learn about aspects of history and culture that may receive scant attention in textbooks. As scholar Eric Foner notes, American history "has been constructed not only in congressional debates and political treatises, but also on plantations and picket lines, in parlors and bedrooms. Frederick Douglass, Eugene V. Debs, and Margaret Sanger . . . are its architects as well as Thomas Jefferson and Abraham Lincoln." While not all

American social movements garner popular support or lead to epoch-changing legislation, they each offer their own unique insight into a young democracy's political dialogue.

Each book in Greenhaven's American Social Movements series allows readers to follow the general progression of a particular social movement—examining its historical roots and beginnings in earlier chapters and relatively recent and contemporary information (or even the movement's demise) in later chapters. With the incorporation of both primary and secondary sources, as well as writings by both supporters and critics of the movement, each anthology provides an engaging panoramic view of its subject. Selections include a variety of readings, such as book excerpts, newspaper articles, speeches, manifestos, literary essays, interviews, and personal narratives. The editors of each volume aim to include the voices of movement leaders and participants as well as the opinions of historians, social analysts, and individuals who have been affected by the movement. This comprehensive approach gives students the opportunity to view these movements both as participants have experienced them and as historians and critics have interpreted them.

Every volume in the American Social Movements series includes an introductory essay that presents a broad historical overview of the movement in question. The annotated table of contents and comprehensive index help readers quickly locate material of interest. Each selection is preceded by an introductory paragraph that summarizes the article's content and provides historical context when necessary. Several other research aids are also present, including brief excerpts of supplementary material, a chronology of major events pertaining to the movement, and an accessible bibliography.

The Greenhaven Press American Social Movements series offers readers an informative introduction to some of the most fascinating groups and ideas in American history. The contents of each anthology provide a valuable resource for general readers as well as for enthusiasts of American political science, history, and culture.

INTRODUCTION

Environmentalism is advocacy for the protection of nature. Usually but not always this means the protection of those areas outside highly developed urban landscapes. Though the environmental movement in America encompasses many contradictory ideas, these ideas nonetheless have at least one element in common: All attempt to answer the question of how humans should interact with the world around them.

OLD WORLD VERSUS NEW WORLD TRADITIONS

The first colonists who migrated to the New World from Europe believed the natural world existed for the benefit of humans. The New World offered plenty of land for farming, abundant firewood, and seemingly endless forests that were rich sources of food and building materials. The Europeans essentially envisioned land use and settlement based on European models. They set about establishing permanent towns and practicing managed agriculture; even forested open land was appreciated for its resemblance to the vast hunting grounds of European nobility.

Native American tribes also intensely exploited natural resources but differently. Some tribes engaged in limited agriculture, other more nomadic tribes in hunting and gathering. Indians also regularly burned the forests. By firing large stretches of forest, Indians assured themselves a stream of deer, moose, and other foraging species that ate the tender shoots of grass that sprang up after the trees had been cleared. Moreover, the fires reduced underbrush, making it easier for the hunter to see his prey. The space cleared by burning made it easier for villagers to detect the approach of foes bent on a surprise attack. For those Indians who farmed, the ash left by burning the forest fertilized indigenous crops such as corn, squash, and beans.

No matter how the Indians worked the land, their exploitation of the environment never approached that of the European colonists, and this disparity lay at the heart of the colonists' claim to the land. English philosopher John Locke argued that ownership of land rested on intensity of use (and thus "improvement" of the land). When different parties claimed the same land, Locke believed the state was justified in awarding ownership to the claimant who either improved the land with the most labor or labored on the land for the longest period of time. In this argument rested the moral justification for European colonization. Native Americans worked large areas of land lightly and irregularly. Conversely, the English lavished hard labor on small, permanent plots. Morally it seemed clear to the English that the vast lonely stretches of forest, mountains, and plains in the New World should go to the Europeans, who nurtured a driving ambition to develop the land to its highest potential.

Philosophy provided the legal basis for European claims to land, but lifestyle also played a crucial role in Europeans' perception of natives and their existing claims. Hunting and gathering and slash-and-burn agriculture require large land areas to support a single tribe. European explorers and settlers saw in North America a largely empty continent and were inspired to claim the seemingly empty land for the English, French, or Spanish Crowns.

Eventually, enough colonists settled along the eastern margin of North America that this onetime wilderness began to feel crowded. As settlers pushed west, they brought their land-use philosophy with them. The principle that land must be owned by someone and intensely used, enshrined in British law, was incorporated in American legal codes. Land was either owned by the state or by private citizens. However, the federal government owned most of its land temporarily because citizens wanted the government to privatize land, not own it; to give it away, not protect it.

Although few questioned the rightness of exploiting natural resources, *how* best to exploit them involved issues of competition, control, and eventually depletion. Forests, for example, were valuable when located near markets where wood could be sold, or along rivers where logs could be floated downriver to a sawmill. The development of railroads changed this picture. Tracts of timber far from large rivers could be tapped for the first time. With the advent of the railways in the 1830s and 1840s lumber could be shipped to markets far from the source, and the timber industry mushroomed, largely unregulated.

Eventually, with the diminution of the forests and the expansion of urban areas, some observers began questioning the wisdom of the unfettered exploitation of nature. Franklin Hough, America's first federal forest agent, argued that forests were not waste lands but valuable public property deserving protection. Charles Sargent published an influential magazine, *Garden and Forest,* that brought public attention to the rapid disappearance of forests and ancient species like the majestic redwoods in California. Soon the voices of scientists joined in calling for conservation.

In the late 1800s naturalist George Perkins Marsh argued that deforestation caused less rainfall. Many streams in the northeast were drying up, with major rivers increasingly sluggish, he noted. Marsh raised the alarming specter of a United States someday as arid as the Mediterranean region if forests continued to be destroyed. Marsh suggested that the extensive root systems of trees helped water seep slowly into the soil, from which it seeped slowly into streams. In addition, trees released water into the atmosphere, where it gathered into clouds and eventually returned to earth in the form of rainfall. By this mechanism, Marsh taught, adequate rainfall and even moderate temperatures could be preserved if Americans protected forests.

But there were other reasons to protect forests besides the regulation of soil erosion, temperature, and rainfall. As America grew, large tracts of wilderness were transformed into urban areas. As American industry and population increased, so too did the need for fuel, in the form of wood. By the mid- to late 1800s, for the first time in American history, the possibility of timber shortages loomed.

Setting aside forests for preservation, however, involved many difficulties. First, the United States could ill afford to slow its economy by cutting fuel supplies. Furthermore, the growing population created a growing demand for farmland. Finally, Americans were accustomed to the idea that they could do as they pleased either on their own land or on public lands. Settlers living near government-owned forests considered it their right as citizens to gather forest products, either hunting, grazing, tapping into trees for resins, or felling trees whole.

EARLY DEVELOPMENT OF MULTIUSE FORESTS

Some states had in fact set aside small areas for protection, and the federal government designated Yellowstone as the first national park in 1872. But Yellowstone was exceptional, in that its unique vistas and geysers made public support easier to win. The effect of Yellowstone on forest conservation was, surprisingly, negative. Senators of western states in particular were reluctant to see forests in their states "locked up" like Yellowstone.

Conservationists thus were faced with a dilemma. They knew that forests needed to be preserved, but they saw that a majority of society had a stake in their exploitation. The solution proved to be simple but profound: Give everyone in society a stake in forest preservation by creating multiuse forests. The model for the multiuse forest was already successfully developed and in practice in the British colonies, particularly India. Why not apply the idea in the United States?

A multiuse forest is a forest set aside by the state to fulfill a number of functions. Unlike a park on the order of Yellowstone, where every natural feature is protected, a multiuse forest is managed in such a way that timber can be harvested. Trees are replanted, and harvests are scheduled according to cycles deemed healthy for the soil and for the protection of the climate and water flow. Nearby residents can obtain permits to graze cattle or sheep or gather firewood for personal use. Camping is usually allowed, as is hunting or fishing, but all must first seek the permission of the ranger who manages the forest.

This model of forest protection gave almost all in society guidelines and incentives to protect forest areas without fear of having individual interest ignored. Seeing a wide constituency served by multiuse forests convinced officials, led first by President Grover Cleveland and then Theodore Roosevelt, to set aside millions of acres of forestland for conservation. Gifford Pinchot, first chief of the U.S. Forest Service, summed up the philosophy underlying the new conservation policy as "the greatest good to the greatest number for the longest time."

EXPANDING THE SCOPE OF CONSERVATIONISM

Conservationists, having found a way to coordinate their interests with those of developers and industrialists, were largely content with existing public policy until well into the twentieth century. Meanwhile, another approach to the environment gained force. Whereas the conservation movement emphasized the dangers of resource depletion, the modern environmental movement took a broader view, including wildlife protection, pollution control, recreation, health promotion, and the value of preserving nature for its own sake. This wider view, originating in the nineteenth century, gained greater prominence after World War II.

The two approaches were not mutually exclusive, and many environmentalists found common ground with traditional conservationists. John Muir was one such environmentalist. He agreed with Gifford Pinchot that many forests should be exploited, and that natural resources had to serve human needs. But Muir also believed that special parks were needed to protect areas merely for their natural beauty. On these grounds, Muir fought—unsuccessfully—Gifford Pinchot and federal agency plans to dam the Hetch Hetchy Valley in California, claiming that the priceless beauty of the valley overrode the need of people in San Francisco for more water.

Federal environmental policy sometimes mirrored this conflict between Pinchot's utilitarian philosophy of land use and

Muir's romantic vision. Though many individuals in the Forest Service shared Muir's perspective, the Forest Service reflected congressional views that America's forests were ultimately a timber, grazing, and mining resource. Congress mandated for the Park Service the mission of preserving nature in a pristine state.

ENVIRONMENTAL CRISES SPUR ACTIVISM

By the 1930s events seemed to be confirming environmentalists' fears. The Plains states were in the grip of an extended drought, and erosion of topsoil brought on by years of intense farming drove thousands of farmers off the land. In response to the situation, a group of midwestern scientists began constructing ecological theories to explain the phenomena of soil erosion, and seek solutions that would take into account not just the need for farmers to continue earning a living from the land, but also the importance of preserving the soil indefinitely.

Frederick Clements, at the University of Kansas, building on the work of A.G. Tansley at Oxford University in Britain, asserted that conservation depended on an understanding of ecology. By this he meant that not only are living species interrelated but that crises in the natural world are linked to multiple, zone-specific factors such as climate, biodiversity, and resource depletion. The dust bowl could thus be better understood as a result of overfarming that had ignored how soil in a particular region interrelated with natural plant life.

By the late 1940s stronger voices in the environmental movement emphasized the need for ecological solutions to problems of conservation. Although conservationists had for decades been balancing a utilitarian view with a broader concern for the aesthetic benefits of wilderness, the effects of growing urbanization, pollution, overpopulation, artificial fertilizers, pesticides, and resource and species depletion mandated greater attention to the interaction of all these factors on the whole web of life. Ecology now came to occupy a larger place in the American consciousness.

For one small group of Americans, a concern for ecology

was nothing new. Organic farmers had for generations claimed that fruits and vegetables grown with chemical fertilizers and protected from insects by pesticides were providing inadequate nutrition and were actually harming humans because of lingering residues of toxins such as DDT and arsenic. These concerns were enough to convince Congress to pass a 1958 law, known as the Delaney Clause, that prohibited the sale of food where reasonable cause existed that it contained substances that caused cancer. But what might have remained a concern mostly of a small number of gardeners received an electrifying boost from the book *Silent Spring* by Rachel Carson, published in 1962.

In her book, Carson raised an alarm about the dangers of pesticides on crops, in particular, about concentrations of pesticide residues killing bird populations. She warned that pesticides traveled up the food chain to poison and disrupt the balance of nature. Unless the government took action to curtail the use of deadly chemicals, human health, and the environment as a whole, would suffer.

THE ENVIRONMENTAL PROTECTION AGENCY IS FOUNDED

As public concern grew about the effects of pesticides on the environment, many ecologists noted the negative effects that other human actions had on the environment. This concern led to increased federal legislation, new government agencies, and the growth of nonprofit public issue groups that characterize the postwar period of environmental history in the United States. In 1969, Congress passed a law that required an environmental impact statement for all major federal construction projects. In the 1970s Congress responded to pressure from environmental groups by passing the Clean Air Act, the Endangered Species Act, the National Environmental Policy Act, the Resource Conservation and Recovery Act, and the Toxic Substances Control Act. These laws marked a period of intense scrutiny by the government over issues of health, pollution, and preservation.

Noting the need for a federal agency to oversee the management of environmental protection efforts, Congress mandated the formation of the Environmental Protection Agency to monitor air pollution control efforts, solid waste management, water pollution, and pesticide use. In issuing permits, assessing and collecting fines, and monitoring and enforcing compliance with federal regulations, the EPA placed environmental concerns at the forefront of public consciousness.

Meanwhile, more or less radical nongovernmental organizations seeking to protect the environment also influenced both public policy and public discourse. The Sierra Club, the Wilderness Society, the Defenders of Wildlife, Greenpeace, and Earth First! all have played a pivotal role in the formation of environmental policy. Through lobbying legislators and grass-roots political organizing, these groups have helped get laws passed to protect old-growth forests, promote international treaties to prohibit whale hunting, and bring the need to control population to the attention of many governments around the world.

Deep Ecology

While resource depletion remained the paramount expression of environmentalism in the 1980s and 1990s, one concern has been increasingly emphasized: deep ecology. This term refers to the belief that our ecological concerns must go beyond the protection of nature for human benefit. Nature exists for its own sake, and has the same ethical right to exist and flourish as humans.

This position is emphasized in the writing of poets like Gary Snyder and philosophers like Arne Naess. With overpopulation and global development threatening the very existence of forests in the Southern Hemisphere, the decline of bird populations observable in one generation, the disappearance of a sizable percentage of species of both plants and animals every year, the greenhouse effect, and ozone layer depletion, environmental activists in the United States, like their peers in other countries, are asserting a more radical ethical imperative. The crisis calls for a rethinking of a utilitarian approach, and the creation of protective structures for nature that may have little or no immediate benefit to human society.

In the last decade of the twentieth century, deep ecology inspired a global political consciousness, the green movement. In the United States the green movement includes a wide range of political and social philosophies, including ecofeminism, the belief that the dominion and exploitation of nature arise from patriarchy; social ecology, the belief that individuals make the greatest change when they work in local communities and neighborhoods; and Gaia worship (*gaia* is Greek for "earth"), which replaces a transcendent God for a female earth deity in the belief that earth as a whole is a living organism. The green movement in the United States has spawned a political party that some feel had a significant effect on the outcome of the 2000 presidential election. The Green Party holds that environmentalism is not an "issue" but an ethical view that replaces liberalism, conservatism, and socialism. Nature should be protected for its own sake, and the political system should incorporate a green ethic into all decision making.

At the dawn of the twenty-first century, the concerns of America's environmentalists are related to those of conservationists of the nineteenth century. Modern environmentalists continue to worry that deforestation will have a long-term negative impact on global climate, soil erosion, and water flow. Americans still fiercely disagree over particular environmental legislation. Consensus on environmental issues is almost impossible to read. Nevertheless, during the last two centuries Americans have asked, "How should we live in relationship to our environment?" Slowly, and progressing by fits and starts Americans have evolved an answer: "Responsibly."

CHAPTER 1

THE AMERICANS AND THEIR LANDSCAPE

Native Americans Changed the Forests to Suit Their Needs

WILLIAM CRONON

In this piece William Cronon describes how Native Americans in southern New England manipulated the environment to suit their needs. This manipulation was accomplished largely by burning vast tracts of forestland. The burning off of underbrush, saplings, and sometimes the whole forest canopy allowed for greater visibility, a parklike setting of meadow and woodland, and superior feeding for game, including deer, elk, turkey, and pheasant, among other animals. The changes in the environment acted as an open invitation to English settlers, who saw the New England forest as a gigantic and inviting park, similar to the managed woodlands in England.

The relationship of the southern New England Indians to their environment was thus, if anything, even more complicated than that of the northern Indians. To the seasons of hunting and fishing shared by both groups were added the agricultural cycles which increased the available food surplus and so enabled denser populations to sustain themselves. In both areas, the mobility of village sites and the shift between various subsistence bases reduced potential strains on any particular segment of the ecosystem, keeping the overall human burden low. But in clearing land for planting and thus concentrating the food base, southern Indians were taking a most important step in reshaping and manipulating the ecosystem.

Clearing fields was relatively easy. By setting fire to wood piled around the base of standing trees, Indian women destroyed the bark and so killed the trees; the women could then plant corn amid the leafless skeletons that were left. During the next several years, many of the trees would topple and could be entirely removed by burning. As one Indian remembered, "An industrious woman, when great many dry logs are fallen, could burn off as many logs in one day as a smart man can chop in two or three days time with an axe." However efficient they were at such clearing, Indian women were frugal with their own labor, and sought to avoid even this much work for as long as they could. That meant returning to the same field site for as long as possible, usually eight to ten years. In time, the soil gradually lost its fertility and eventually necessitated movement to a new field. (Soil exhaustion was to some extent delayed by the action of the nitrogen-fixing beans which Indian women planted with the corn; whether they were aware of it or not, this was one of the side benefits of planting multicrop fields.)

HEAVY HUMAN USE

The annual reoccupation of fixed village and planting sites meant that the area around field and camp experienced heavy human use: intensive food gathering, the accumulation of garbage, and, most importantly, the consumption of firewood. One of the main reasons Indians moved to winter camps was that their summer sites had been stripped of the fuel essential for winter fires. Indians believed in big fires—one colonist said that "their Fire is instead of our bed cloaths"—and burned wood heavily all night long, both summer and winter. Such practices could not long be maintained on a single site. As Morton said, "They use not to winter and summer in one place, for that would be a reason to make fuell scarce." The Indians were thus no strangers to the fuel shortages so familiar to the English, even if Indian scarcities were more local. When Verrazzano found twenty-five to thirty leagues of treeless land in Narragansett Bay, or Higginson spoke of thousands of acres in a similar state near Boston, they were observing the effects of agricultural Indians returning to fixed village sites and so consuming their forest energy supply. Indeed, when the Indians wondered why English colonists were coming to their land, the first explanation that occurred to them was a fuel shortage. Roger Williams recounted:

> This question they oft put to me: Why come the *Englishmen* hither? and measuring others by themselves; they say, It is because you want *firing:* for they, having burnt up the *wood* in one place, (wanting draughts [animals] to bring *wood* to them) they are faine to follow the *wood;* and so to remove to a fresh new place for the *woods* sake.

Williams regarded this merely as a quaint instance of Indian provincialism, but in one ironic sense, given what we know of the English forests of the seventeenth century, the Indians were perhaps shrewder than he knew.

The effect of southern New England Indian villages on their environment was not limited to clearing fields or stripping forests for firewood. What most impressed English visitors was the Indians' burning of extensive sections of the surrounding forest once or twice a year. "The Salvages," wrote Thomas Morton, "are accustomed to set fire of the Country in all places where they come, and to burne it twize a yeare, viz: at the Spring, and the fall of the leafe." Here was the reason that the southern forests were so open and parklike; not because the trees naturally grew thus, but because the Indians preferred them so. As William Wood observed, the fire "consumes all the underwood and rubbish which otherwise would overgrow the country, making it unpassable, and spoil their much affected hunting." The result was a forest of large, widely spaced trees, few shrubs, and much grass and herbage. "In those places where the Indians inhabit," said Wood, "there is scarce a bush or bramble or any cumbersome underwood to be seen in the more champion ground." By removing underwood and fallen trees, the Indians reduced the total accumulated fuel at ground level. With only small nonwoody plants to consume, the annual fires moved quickly, burned with relatively low temperatures, and soon extinguished themselves. They were more

Contrasting colonists' permanent settlements, Roger Williams observed Native Americans' manipulation of the environment through controlled burnings, multicrop fields, and seasonal migration.

ground fires than forest fires, not usually involving larger trees, and so they rarely grew out of control. Fires of this kind could be used to drive game for hunting, to clear fields for planting, and, on at least one occasion, to fend off European invaders.

Northern Indians do not appear to have engaged in such burning. Because they did not practice agriculture and so were less tied to particular sites, they had less incentive to alter the environment of a given spot. Their chief mode of transportation was the canoe, so that they had less need of an open forest for traveling. Moreover, many of the northern tree species were not well adapted to repeated burning, and northern forests tended to accumulate enough fuel at ground level that, once a fire got started, it usually reached the canopy and burned out of control. Conditions in southern New England were quite different. Denser, fixed settlements encouraged heavy use of more limited forest areas, and most inland travel was by land. The trees of the southern forest, once fully grown, suffered little more than charred bark if subjected to ground fires of short duration. If destroyed, they regenerated themselves by sprouting from their roots: chestnuts, oaks, and hickories, the chief constituents of the southern upland forests, are in fact sometimes known as "sprout hardwoods." Repeated fires tended to destroy trees and shrubs which lacked this ability, including hemlock, beech, and juniper. Even the white pine, which often sprang up after large forest fires, tended be killed off if subjected to regular burning because of its inability to sprout, and so was uncommon in the vicinity of active Indian settlements.

Colonial observers understood burning as being part of Indian efforts to simplify hunting and facilitate travel; most failed to see its subtler ecological effects. In the first place, it increased the rate at which forest nutrients were recycled into the soil, so that grasses, shrubs, and nonwoody plants tended to grow more luxuriantly following a fire than they had before. Especially on old Indian fields, fire created conditions favorable to strawberries, blackberries, raspberries, and other gatherable foods. Grasses like the little bluestem were rare in a mature forest, but in a forest burned by Indians they became abundant. The thinning of the forest canopy, which resulted from the elimination of smaller trees, allowed more light to reach the forest floor and further aided such growth. The soil became warmer and drier, discouraging tree species which preferred moister conditions—beech, sugar maple, red maple, black birch—and favoring drier species like oaks when regular burning was allowed to lapse. Burning also tended to destroy plant diseases and pests, not to mention the fleas which inevitably became abundant around Indian settlements. Roger Williams summed up these effects by commenting that "this burning of the Wood to them they count a Benefit, both for destroying of vermin, and keeping downe the Weeds and thickets."

A MOSAIC OF ECOSYSTEMS

Selective Indian burning thus promoted the mosaic quality of New England ecosystems, creating forests in many different states of ecological succession. In particular, regular fires promoted what ecologists call the "edge effect." By encouraging the growth of extensive regions which resembled the boundary areas between forests and grasslands, Indians created ideal habitats for a host of wildlife species. Of all early American observers, only the astute Timothy Dwight seems to have commented on this phenomenon. "The object of these conflagrations," he wrote, "was to produce fresh and sweet pasture for the purpose of alluring the deer to the spots on which they had been kindled." The effect was even subtler than Dwight realized: because the enlarged edge areas actually raised the total herbivorous food supply, they not merely attracted game but helped create much larger populations of it. Indian burning promoted the increase of exactly those species whose abundance so impressed English colonists: elk, deer, beaver, hare, porcupine, turkey, quail, ruffed grouse, and so on. When these populations increased, so did the carnivorous eagles, hawks, lynxes, foxes, and wolves. In short, Indians who hunted game animals were not just taking the "unplanted bounties of nature"; in an important sense, they were harvesting a foodstuff which they had consciously been instrumental in creating.

Few English observers could have realized this. People accustomed to keeping domesticated animals lacked the conceptual tools to realize that Indians were practicing a more distant kind of husbandry of their own. To the colonists, only Indian women appeared to do legitimate work; the men idled away their time in hunting, fishing, and wantonly burning the woods, none of which seemed like genuinely productive activities to Europeans. English observers often commented about how hard Indian women worked. "It is almost incredible," Williams wrote, "what burthens the poore women carry of *Corne*, of *Fish*, of *Beanes*, of *Mats*, and a childe besides." The criticism of Indian males in such remarks was usually explicit. "Their wives are their slaves," wrote Christopher Levett, "and do all the work; the men will do nothing but kill beasts, fish, etc." For their part, Indian men seemed to acknowledge that their wives were a principal source of wealth and mocked Englishmen for not working their wives harder. According to the lawyer Thomas Lechford, "They say, *Englishman* much

the wheel of the seasons: throughout New England, Indians held their demands on the ecosystem to a minimum by moving their settlements from habitat to habitat. As one of the earliest European visitors noted, "They move . . . from one place to another according to the richness of the site and the season." By using other species when they were most plentiful, Indians made sure that no single species became overused. It was a way of life to match the patchwork of the landscape. On the coast were fish and shellfish, and in the salt marshes were migratory birds. In the forests and lowland thickets were deer and beaver; in cleared upland fields were corn and beans; and everywhere were the wild plants whose uses were too numerous to catalog. For New England Indians, ecological diversity, whether natural or artificial, meant abundance, stability, and a regular supply of the things that kept them alive.

The ecological relationships which the English sought to reproduce in New England were no less cyclical than those of the Indians; they were only simpler and more concentrated. The English too had their seasons of want and plenty, and rapidly adjusted their false expectations of perpetual natural wealth to match New World realities. But whereas Indian villages moved from habitat to habitat to find maximum abundance through minimal work, and so reduce their impact on the land, the English believed in and required permanent settlements. Once a village was established, its improvements—cleared fields, pastures, buildings, fences, and so on—were regarded as more or less fixed features of the landscape. English fixity sought to replace Indian mobility; here was the central conflict in the ways Indians and colonists interacted with their environments. The struggle was over two ways of living and using the seasons of the year, and it expressed itself in how two peoples conceived of property, wealth, and boundaries on the landscape.

Farmers Must Protect the Fertility of the Soil

JAMES MADISON

James Madison, the fourth president of the United States, and a leading contributor to the U.S. Constitution, expressed concern about the misuse of the soil by American farmers. Because of the seemingly endless supply of vacant land, and because of the high expense of labor, many farmers found it easier to exhaust the soil on one farm and move on to another. Proper care of farmland included buying or gathering manure, hauling to the field, spreading it over the topsoil and then plowing it in between crops. Madison urged farmers to take a long-range view of farming and to avoid short-term practices that destroyed the productivity of the soil.

I shall venture on the task, a task the least difficult, of pointing out some of the most prevalent errors in our husbandry, and which appear to be among those which may merit the attention of the society, and the instructive examples of its members.

CHEAP LAND, EXPENSIVE LABOR

I. The error first to be noticed is that of cultivating land, either naturally poor or impoverished by cultivation. This error, like many others, is the effect of habit, continued after the reason for it has failed. Whilst there was an abundance of fresh and fertile soil, it was the interest of the cultivator to spread his labor over as great a surface as he could. Land being cheap and labor dear, and the land co-operating powerfully with the la-

Excerpted from "Intelligent Husbandry," by James Madison (1818), as reprinted in *A Documentary History of Conservation in America*, edited by Robert McHenry (New York: Praeger, 1972).

bor, it was profitable to draw as much as possible from the land. Labor is now comparatively cheaper and land dearer. Where labor has risen in price fourfold land has increased tenfold. It might be profitable, therefore, now to contract the surface over which labor is spread, even if the soil retained its freshness and fertility. But this is not the case. Much of the fertile soil is exhausted, and unfertile soils are brought into cultivation; and both cooperating less with labor in producing the crop, it is necessary to consider how far labor can be profitably exerted on them; whether it ought not to be applied towards making them fertile, rather than in further impoverishing them, or whether it might not be more profitably applied to mechanical occupations, or to domestic manufactures?

In the old countries of Europe, where labor is cheap and land dear, the object is to augment labor, and contract the space on which it is employed. In the new settlements taking place in this country, the original practice here may be rationally pursued. In the old settlements, the reason for the practice in Europe is becoming daily less inapplicable; and we ought to yield to the change of circumstances, by forbearing to waste our labor on land which, besides not paying for it, is still more impoverished, and rendered more difficult to be made rich. The crop which is of least amount, gives the blow most mortal to the soil. It has not been a very rare thing to see land under the plough, not producing enough to feed the ploughman and his horse; and it is in such cases that the death blow is given. The goose is killed, without even obtaining the coveted egg.

There cannot be a more rational principle in the code of agriculture, than that every farm which is in good heart should be kept so; that every one not in good heart should be made so; and that what is right as to the farm, generally, is so as to every part of every farm. Any system therefore, or want of system, which tends to make a rich farm poor, or does not tend to make a poor farm rich, cannot be good for the owner; whatever it may be for the tenant or superintendent, who has transient interest only in it. The profit, where there is any, will not balance the loss of intrinsic value sustained by the land.

II. The evil of pressing too hard upon the land, has also been much increased by the bad mode of ploughing it. Shallow ploughing, and ploughing up and down hilly land, have, by exposing the loosened soil to be carried off by rains, has-

James Madison

tened more than any thing else, the waste of its fertility. When the mere surface is pulverized, moderate rains on land but little uneven, if ploughed up and down, gradually wear it away. And heavy rains on hilly land, ploughed in that manner, soon produce a like effect, notwithstanding the improved practice of deeper ploughing. How have the beauty and value of this red ridge of country suffered from this cause? And how much is due to the happy improvement introduced by a member of this society, whom I need not name.* by a cultivation in horizontal drills with a plough adapted to it? Had the practice prevailed from the first settlement of the country, the general fertility would have been more than the double of what the red hills, and indeed all other hilly lands, now possess; and the scars and sores now defacing them would no where be seen. Happily, experience is proving that this remedy, aided by a more rational management in other respects, is adequate to the purpose of healing what has been wounded, as well as of preserving the health of what has escaped the calamity. It is truly gratifying to observe how fast the improvement is spreading from the parent example. The value of our red hills, under a mode of cultivation which guards their fertility against wasting rains, is probably exceeded by that of no uplands whatever;

*Col. T.M. Randolph

and without that advantage they are exceeded in value by almost all others. They are little more than a lease for years.

Besides the inestimable advantage from horizontal ploughing, in protecting the soil against the wasting effect of rains, there is a great one in its preventing the rains themselves from being lost to the crop. The Indian corn is the crop which most exposes the soil to be carried off by the rains; and it is at the same time the crop which most needs them. Where the land is not only hilly, but the soil thirsty, (as is the case particularly throughout this mountainous range,) the preservation of the rain as it falls, between the drilled ridges, is of peculiar importance; and its gradual settling downwards to the roots, is the best possible mode of supplying them with moisture. In the old method of ploughing shallow, with the furrows up and down, the rain as well as the soil was lost.

Restoring Fertility

III. The neglect of manures is another error which claims particular notice. It may be traced to the same cause with our excessive cropping. In the early stages of our agriculture, it was more convenient, and more profitable, to bring new land into cultivation, than to improve exhausted land. The failure of new land has long called for the improvement of old land; but habit has kept us deaf to the call.

Nothing is more certain than that continual cropping without manure, deprives the soil of its fertility. It is equally certain that fertility may be preserved or restored, by giving to the earth animal or vegetable manure equivalent to the matter taken from it; and that a perpetual fertility is not, in itself, incompatible with an uninterrupted succession of crops. The Chinese, it is said, smile at the idea, that land needs rest, as if like animals it had a sense of fatigue. Their soil does not need rest, because an industrious use is made of every fertilizing particle that can contribute towards replacing what has been drawn from it. And this is the more practicable with them, as almost the whole of what is grown on their farms is consumed within them. That a restoration to the earth of all that annually grows on it, prevents its impoverishment, is sufficiently seen in our forests, where the annual exuviae of the trees and plants replace the fertility of which they deprive the earth. Where frequent fires destroy the leaves and whatever else is annually dropped on the earth, it is well known that the land becomes poorer: this destruction of the natural crop, having the same impoverishing effect, as a removal of a cultivated crop. A still stronger proof that an animal restoration to the earth of all its annual product will perpetuate its productiveness, is seen where our fields are left uncultivated and unpastured. In this case the soil, receiving from the decay of the spontaneous weeds and grasses more fertility than they extract from it, is for a time at least improved, not impoverished. Its improvement may be explained, by the fertilizing matter which the weeds and grasses derive from water and the atmosphere, which forms a net gain to the earth. At what point, or from what cause, the formation and accumulation of vegetable mould from this gain ceases, is not perhaps very easy to be explained. That it does cease, is proved by the stationary condition of the surface of the earth in old forests; and that the amount of the accumulation varies with the nature of the subjacent earth, is equally certain. It seems to depend also on the species of trees and plants which happen to contribute the materials for the vegetable mould.

But the most eligible mode of preserving the richness, and of enriching the poverty of a farm, is certainly that of applying to the soil a sufficiency of animal and vegetable matter in a putrefied state or a state ready for putrefaction; in order to procure which, too much care cannot be observed in saving every material furnished by the farm. This resource was among the earliest discoveries of men living by agriculture; and a proper use of it has been made a test of good husbandry, in all countries, ancient and modern, where its principles and profits have been studied.

Colonists' Views of Forests Changed over Time

MICHAEL WILLIAMS

Michael Williams discusses how Europeans reacted to the monumental American forests—both their extent and its density. Reactions of European settlers to the forest were many: repugnance, due in part to the dangers found in the forests; attraction, due to the romantic allure of scenic beauty; suspicion, due to their association of the forest with pagan practices and peoples; and utilization, since the Europeans saw that the wilderness could be put to use. This selection helps explain the feelings and ideas behind the felling of the great American forests. Michael Williams is considered the world's leading forest historian and teaches at Oriel College, Oxford University.

To the early American pioneers the forest was repugnant, forbidding, and repulsive. Some of those feelings and reactions had roots that went back a long way, into the culture of their ancestors in Europe, but were to be reenacted in a dialogue between the European pioneer's mind and the American environment. In Europe from classical times to post-medieval times society had developed a mythology and set of cultural mores in relation to the extensive forests of the Continent. The forests were the wild areas, alien to man and in need to felling, firing, grazing, and cultivating so that they could become civilized abodes. The forests were dark and horrible places where there were very real dangers from wild animals, particularly bears and wolves. The word "wilderness" was almost synonymous with forest; etymologically, it was the

Excerpted from *Americans and Their Forests: A Historical Geography*, by Michael Williams. Copyright © Cambridge University Press 1989. Reprinted with permission from Cambridge University Press.

THE AMERICANS AND THEIR LANDSCAPE • 35

"place of wild beasts." In addition, the forests were places of terrifying eeriness, awe, and horror, where the imagination played tricks and the limbs of the trees looked like the limbs of people, especially if animated by the wind. In that chaos the hapless peasant was first *be-wildered* and eventually succumbed to license and sin. . . .

AN ENEMY TO BE CONQUERED

The sinister and frightening image of the forest meant that it was portrayed as the "enemy" that needed to be "conquered." However, the dangers of the forest were real enough. It was the haunt of wild animals; few matters took up so much space in the records of the inland towns of New England during the early seventeenth century as the killing and maiming of live-stock by wild animals. The terror of the forest was reinforced during King Philip's uprising when nature itself seemed to contrive to help the Indians in their attacks on the colonists so that, said Increase Mather, "Our men when in that hideous place, if they but see a Bush stir, would fire presently, whereby it is verily feared they did sometimes unhappily shoot Men in-stead of Indians." The Indians seemed to appear from behind trees to attack and then melt away into the darkness of the for-est. But the forest also had a symbolic meaning. It was the dark and sinister symbol of man's evil, where one was beyond the reach of redemption and where even a civilized man could re-vert to savagery if left too long. The fact that the Indian in-habited the forest and did not appear to clear it seemed proof enough of that. . . .

Above all, it was the size of the forest that astonished and frustrated the New World pioneers, especially after the expe-rience of the transatlantic journey, which was often terrifying enough. The forest was impersonal and lonely in its endless-ness; consequently, clearing the forest was likened to a battle or struggle between the individual and the immense obstacle that had to be overcome in order to create a new life and a new society. The image of the heroic struggle to subdue the sullen and unyielding forest by the hand of man, and to make it something better than it was, was a legacy of feeling, thought, and imagery that was handed down over the centuries. For Francis Parkman in 1885 the forest was "an enemy to be overcome by any means, fair or foul," and Frederick Jackson Turner, the inheritor and brilliantly successful interpreter of these deeply held images, echoed these ideas and attitudes in his account of early pioneer life. The frontier was the ultimate American symbol and the place where the pioneer created the world anew. . . .

IMPROVING THE LAND

Writing about his life in the northwestern portion of New York State in the late eighteenth century, William Cooper declared that his "great primary aim" was "to cause the wilderness to bloom and fructify." Because of these and similar attitudes, the landscape of "unimproved land" was a desirable aim. From 1860 onward and without interruption to the present day, these two categories of land have been recorded in the censuses, the amount of "improved land" being one of the main criteria of material progress in rural America. To fell the forest was almost to enter the kingdom of heaven on earth, as the making of new land seemed to demonstrate the direct causal relationship between moral effort, sobriety, frugality, and industry and material reward. Increasingly, American nature seemed full of implications for ethical and material betterment. Very early in the eighteenth century, Franklin identified the frontier of cultivation with opportunity and "tended to measure moral and spiritual progress by progress in converting the wilderness into a paradise of material plenty." Half-playfully, he even attributed a cosmic influence to the clearing of the forest: "by *clearing America* of Woods" Americans were "*Scouring our Planet* . . . and so making this Side of our Globe reflect a brighter Light to the Eyes of the Inhabitants of *Mars* or *Venus.*" The link with virtue was pointed out explicitly in Andrew Jackson's second annual address, in which he asked rhetorically,

What good man would prefer a country covered with

forests, and ranged by a few thousand savages to our extensive Republic, studded with cities, towns, and prosperous farms, embellished with all the improvements which art can devise or industry execute, occupied by more than 12,000,000 happy people, and filled with all the blessings of liberty, civilization, and religion?

If the forest and the Indian were swept aside in the process, then so be it. Not only progress was good; it was also inevitable. . . .

Generally, hostility and repugnance toward the forest remained because the bulk of the population was still confronting it and clearing it, but the forest began to find new champions among those who found aesthetic values in it and even associated its primitive, primordial condition with the works of God, which, if we consider all that had gone before, was an intellectual revolution. Like most other intellectual revolutions, this changed attitude was not a sudden eruption of ideas; rather, it was a gradual fermentation of ideas that had been current for a long time but were now formulated and articulated with greater clarity. . . .

When William Penn wrote in 1688, "The country life is to be preferred for there we see the works of God, but in the Cities little else but the works of man," he was extolling the virtues of the made landscape and the rural pioneer life—its simplicity, sobriety, frugality, tranquillity, freshness, and the regenerative powers of the cycles of nature; he was not extolling the qualities of the pristine forest. It was no accident that two other major figures in American history and pioneer life expounded similar ideas about the agrarian ideal. In America, Thomas Jefferson wrote, "We have an immensity of land courting the industry of the husbandman." Why, then, turn to manufacturing, especially since "Those who labor in the earth are the chosen people of God, if ever He had a chosen people, whose breasts he has made his peculiar deposit for substantial and genuine virtue"? For Benjamin Franklin, agriculture was the only "honest" way of acquiring wealth, and, moreover, it kept people virtuous and morally righteous. Undoubtedly, the spectre of the growing power and complexity of industry and mechanization, and the intrusion of the urban into the rural during the opening years of the nineteenth century, perturbed those who saw the rural ideal being destroyed and the beginning of disharmony between man and nature. Washington Irving summed up the feeling well in *The Legend of Sleepy Hollow,* written in 1820:

> I mention this peaceful spot with all possible laud; for it is in such little retired . . . valleys that population, manners, and customs remain fixed; while the great torrent of migration and improvement, which is making such incessant change in other parts of this restless country, sweeps by them unobserved. They are little nooks of still water which border a rapid stream.

A New Meaning for Forests

The romantic movement gave the forests a new meaning for some people, and this admiration for what had once been rejected was bolstered by yet another change of attitude, which can best be called the "patriotic." After the War of Independence the question was continually asked, "What was it in this new country that was distinctively American?" The continent, with its short history and ill-formed traditions, could not produce anything like the rich cultural heritage and the antiquities of Europe. One thing that America had, however, was vast areas of untouched land—forest, prairie, and mountain—and these seemingly unending wild areas were perceived by nineteenth-century naturalists, poets, writers, and artists as something uniquely American and something about which to be proud. Chateaubriand touched upon this feeling when he said, "There is nothing old in America excepting the woods. . . . they are certainly the equivalent for monuments and ancestors." The naturalists and diarists had led the way in spreading "a proper feeling of nationality," but the "boundless," "trackless," "incomparable," and "fresh" forests also became the object of literary and artistic attention and pride. The writing of Washington Irving, the poems of William Cullen Bryant ("A Forest Hymn," 1825) and James Kirk Paulding ("The Backwoodsman," 1818), and above all, the Leatherstocking novels of James Fenimore Cooper, written between 1823 and 1841, produced a new appreciation of the forest landscapes of the country and a pride and confidence in the qualities of the American scene. The literary appreciation was paralleled by the visual appreciation, and Thomas Cole, in particular, the leader of the Hudson River school of painting that flourished during the 1830s and 1840s, reveled in the wildness of American scenery (of the forested Catskills in particular) and indicated it as a subject worthy of study and reproduction.

The new appreciation, let it be admitted, was not wholly affirmative. Feelings of disgust and fear of the forest still come through, and feelings of pride and satisfaction in the pioneer endeavor to clear and settle the forests were also strong. After all, the process of subjecting the wild landscape to the plow produced the self-dependence, simplicity, manliness, and neighborliness of the American people. This ambivalence about the forests was rarely absent. Even Emerson, 11 years after he had written, "in the woods we return to reason and faith," could still say:

> This great savage country should be furrowed by the plough and combed by the harrow . . . these rough Alleganies should know their master, these foaming torrents should be bestridden by proud arches of stone; these wild prairies should be loaded with wheat; these swamps with rice; the hill tops should pasture sheep and cattle; the interminable forests should be graceful parks for use and delight.

By the mid-nineteenth century the significance of the uniquely American character of the continent's scenery took another twist with the writing of Emerson and particularly of Thoreau. They both expounded the transcendentalist philosophy that the experience of nature in general, but of the forests in particular, produced a higher awareness and sense of reality than did one's physical surroundings, which were dominated by expansion and exploitation, particularly in the cities, which were "great conspiracies." In other words, nature mirrored God's higher meaning and was not only aesthetically pleasing but positively and rationally beneficial. Unlike the Puritan pioneers who thought that morality stopped on the edge of the clearing, the transcendentalists thought it began there, for man was inherently good and not evil, and perfection could be maximized on entering the forests. By halting stages the argument went further. If the forest and the other wilderness areas were uniquely American, and if God's purpose was made more manifest in such places, then the very spirit of America and its creativity could be found in the forests, from whence came, said Thoreau, "the tonics and barks that brace mankind." Here, perhaps, were some of the intellectual seeds of [Frederick Jackson] Turner's frontier hypothesis, that the "frontier," the "cutting edge" of civilization as it faced the "untouched forest," prairie, or mountain, was the crucible in which were forged the American traits and institutions of self-reliance, industry, and democracy, as people fled from the uniformity and degeneration of the urban areas. Quite simply, for Turner, "American democracy was no theorist's dream . . . it came out of the American Forest."

Thoreau's philosophy had one other effect. He believed that wilderness without the benefits of civilization was detrimental to mankind; therefore, the optimum condition for man was one in which he could participate and keep in contact with both ends of the spectrum. With this view of the binary requirements of man, Thoreau gave the traditional American idealization of the "rural" or pastoral environment a new respectability.

A GROWING SCARCITY

Most Americans thought that the forest and its timber were limitless, but even as early as 1745 Benjamin Franklin was lamenting the scarcity of fuel that had formerly been "at any man's door." Now it had to be brought nearly 100 miles to the large coastal towns, and at considerable cost. By the late eighteenth century the situation was acute, particularly in the urban areas, if the winter was excessively prolonged and cold. By 1840 deficiencies in constructional timber also became evident on the eastern seaboard, and by 1870 New York State was importing from beyond its boundaries over 1 million tons of timber annually.

After the mid-nineteenth century, answers to the problems of deficiencies and high costs were sought in the development of better communications, in order to bring timber to the areas of consumption from the untouched forests farther afield, and in mass production methods to keep down costs. But by the latter years of the century there was also a realization that some form of silviculture was desirable, that is to say, management of the existing forest stand to maximize yield.

Concern over the growing scarcity of timber and fuel was coupled with another worry: What was clearing doing to the land itself? Many late-eighteenth- and early-nineteenth-century writers regarded the New World as a "great outdoor laboratory" for observing scientific changes, for controlling nature and for making it useful. But it remained for George Perkins Marsh to combine the experience of his youth in Vermont, where he saw forest clearing and erosion at first hand, with the well-documented observations of Europe (where he lived in later years) to produce his brilliant synthesis, *Man and Nature; or, Physical Geography as Modified by Human Action,* in 1864, more than one-third of which was devoted to forests and forest influences.

Earlier, in 1847, Marsh had addressed the Rutland agricultural fair. After praising the effort of the pioneer farmers in changing the forest to farmland, he went on to say: "the increasing value of timber and fuel ought to teach us, that the trees are no longer what they were in our fathers' time, an encumberance." But he went beyond economic concerns to elaborate environmental concerns. Already too much of Vermont had been cleared, and every middle-aged man who returned to his birthplace after the interval of a few years would see that "the signs of artificial improvement are mingled with the tokens of improvident waste," such as erosion, ravines, and dried-up streams.

Marsh went beyond the concerns of his contemporaries about conserving wood and increasing yield to consider the wider implications of clearing and of the influence of the forest. He emphasized the destructive powers of man's everyday activities, which upset the "harmonies of nature," and he suggested that wise management could mitigate some of these problems. It was a big step in American and, indeed, world thinking.

The idea that nature was an organic Whole and that the forest influenced other facets of nature had far-reaching effects. The settlers moving into the treeless plains of states such as Kansas and Nebraska during the 1870s wanted to plant trees and increase rainfall. The settlers and irrigators of the arid West, the flood controllers of the East, and those concerned with erosion everywhere wanted positive forest policies. Increasingly, people regretted and resented the devastation wrought by mass production, large-scale lumbering, particularly in the forests of the Great Lakes, which left worthless cutovers. The disquiet about the probable effects of human interference on the influence of the forest on the environment as a whole became a major factor in the public acceptance of forestry.

In his voluminous writing Thoreau constantly decried the felling of the forests, and in *The Maine Woods,* written in 1858, he talked of "our natural preserves" and of the necessity of retaining a portion of that natural environment for posterity. But the concept of preservation was taken one step further by Marsh, who in a later edition of *Man and Nature* in 1874 saw preservation not only as a benefit by nature to man but also as a benefit by man to nature. It was a wider concept of preservation than had been held before, and it emphasized the reciprocal bonds that tied mankind to the environment. To that end he advocated that a "large and easily accessible region should remain, as far as is possible, in its primitive condition." It was the beginning of conservation, and it started in the forest.

From then on the movement to protect that national heritage became intense. There was a growing commitment by the government to preserve and manage forested catchments and other forest areas, with the creation, in time, of federal forest reserves, not only for economic purposes to ensure a supply of timber but also to provide areas of recreational, scenic, and aesthetic value and, later, even to preserve areas of "wilderness." By about 1890 the appreciation of the forest and other wild places had passed from being the concern of a small and articulate group of writers, artists, poets, and politicians to becoming a national cult. For many Americans, who were now urban dwellers, the primitive conditions of nature no longer impinged on their lives and were no longer to be feared. The frontier had passed, and the wild landscape no longer repelled. Such landscapes were now sought out actively, and they could be seen in comparative comfort by the vacationer. In the popular imagination they were now imbued with attributes all of which were good.

Paradoxically, however, the horror of the forest was transferred to the ever-expanding urban areas, which became "concrete jungles" and "asphalt jungles," godless and physically dangerous places where it was possible for one to lose one's identity, morality, sensitivity, and even one's life. An intellectual process was occurring in which the values attributed to the forest and to civilized places were being exchanged. The poles had been reversed.

Mankind Is Inextricably Linked to Nature

RALPH WALDO EMERSON

The American essayist, poet, and philosopher Ralph Waldo Emerson wrote for a wide American audience. Emerson was a member of the Transcendentalist movement, which emphasized individual responsibility, rejected materialism, and advocated a return to nature for spiritual guidance. In the following viewpoint, Emerson espouses the view that all living things are interrelated. Though expressed poetically and mystically, Emerson's ideas are often seen by environmental historians as the philosophical underpinnings of the science of ecology.

The stars awaken a certain reverence, because though always present, they are inaccessible; but all natural objects make a kindred impression, when the mind is open to their influence. Nature never wears a mean appearance. Neither does the wisest man extort her secret, and lose his curiosity by finding out all her perfection. Nature never became a toy to a wise spirit. The flowers, the animals, the mountains, reflected the wisdom of his best hour, as much as they had delighted the simplicity of his childhood. When we speak of nature in this manner, we have a distinct but most poetical sense in the mind. We mean the integrity of impression made by manifold natural objects. It is this which distinguishes the stick of timber of the wood-cutter, from the tree of the poet. The charming landscape which I saw this morning, is indubitably made up of some twenty or thirty farms. Miller owns this field, Locke that,

Excerpted from "Nature," by Ralph Waldo Emerson, www.rwe.org.

and Manning the woodland beyond. But none of them owns the landscape. There is a property in the horizon which no man has but he whose eye can integrate all the parts, that is, the poet. This is the best part of these men's farms, yet to this their warranty-deeds give no title. To speak truly, few adult persons can see nature. Most persons do not see the sun. At least they have a very superficial seeing. The sun illuminates only the eye of the man, but shines into the eye and the heart of the child. The lover of nature is he whose inward and outward senses are still truly adjusted to each other; who has retained the spirit of infancy even into the era of manhood. His intercourse with heaven and earth, becomes part of his daily food. In the presence of nature, a wild delight runs through the man, in spite of real sorrows. Nature says,—he is my creature, and maugre all his impertinent griefs, he shall be glad with me. Not the sun or the summer alone, but every hour and season yields its tribute of delight; for every hour and change corresponds to and authorizes a different state of the mind, from breathless noon to grimmest midnight. Nature is a setting that fits equally well a comic or a mourning piece. In good health, the air is a cordial of incredible virtue. Crossing a bare common, in snow puddles, at twilight, under a clouded sky, without having in my thoughts any occurrence of special good fortune, I have enjoyed a perfect exhilaration. I am glad to the brink of fear. In the woods too, a man casts off his years, as the snake his slough, and at what period soever of life, is always a child. In the woods, is perpetual youth. Within these plantations of God, a decorum and sanctity reign, a perennial festival is dressed, and the guest sees not how he should tire of them in a thousand years. In the woods, we return to reason and faith. There I feel that nothing can befall me in life,—no disgrace, no calamity, (leaving me my eyes,) which nature cannot repair. Standing on the bare ground,—my head bathed by the blithe air, and uplifted into infinite space,—all mean egotism vanishes. I become a transparent eye-ball; I am nothing; I see all; the currents of the Universal Being circulate through me; I am part or particle of God. The name of the nearest friend sounds then foreign and accidental: to be brothers, to be acquaintances,—master or servant, is then a trifle and a disturbance. I am the lover of uncontained and immortal beauty. In the wilderness, I find something more dear and connate than in streets or villages. In the tranquil landscape, and especially in the distant line of the horizon, man beholds somewhat as beautiful as his own nature.

THE DELIGHT OF FIELDS AND WOODS

The greatest delight which the fields and woods minister, is the suggestion of an occult relation between man and the vegetable. I am not alone and unacknowledged. They nod to me, and I to them. The waving of the boughs in the storm, is new to me and old. It takes me by surprise, and yet is not unknown. Its effect is like that of a higher thought or a better emotion coming over me, when I deemed I was thinking justly or doing right.

Yet it is certain that the power to produce this delight, does not reside in nature, but in man, or in a harmony of both. It is necessary to use these pleasures with great temperance. For, nature is not always tricked in holiday attire, but the same scene which yesterday breathed perfume and glittered as for the frolic of the nymphs, is overspread with melancholy today. Nature always wears the colors of the spirit. To a man laboring under calamity, the heat of his own fire hath sadness in it. Then, there is a kind of contempt of the landscape felt by him who has just lost by death a dear friend. The sky is less grand as it shuts down over less worth in the population. . . .

Space, time, society, labor, climate, food, locomotion, the animals, the mechanical forces, give us sincerest lessons, day by day, whose meaning is unlimited. They educate both the Understanding and the Reason. Every property of matter is a school for the understanding,—its solidity or resistance, its inertia, its extension, its figure, its divisibility. The understanding adds, divides, combines, measures, and finds nutriment and room for its activity in this worthy scene. Meantime, Reason transfers all these lessons into its own world of thought, by perceiving the analogy that marries Matter and Mind.

Understanding Intellectual Truths

1. Nature is a discipline of the understanding in intellectual truths. Our dealing with sensible objects is a constant exercise in the necessary lessons of difference, of likeness, of order, of being and seeming, of progressive arrangement; of ascent from particular to general; of combination to one end of manifold forces. Proportioned to the importance of the organ to be formed, is the extreme care with which its tuition is provided,— a care pretermitted in no single case. What tedious training, day after day, year after year, never ending, to form the common sense; what continual reproduction of annoyances, inconveniences, dilemmas; what rejoicing over us of little men; what disputing of prices, what reckonings of interest,—and all to form the Hand of the mind;—to instruct us that "good thoughts are no better than good dreams, unless they be executed!"

The same good office is performed by Property and its filial systems of debt and credit. Debt, grinding debt, whose iron face the widow, the orphan, and the sons of genius fear and hate;—debt, which consumes so much time, which so cripples and disheartens a great spirit with cares that seem so base, is a preceptor whose lessons cannot be forgone, and is needed most by those who suffer from it most. Moreover, property, which has been well compared to snow,—"if it fall level to-day, it will be blown into drifts to-morrow,"—is the surface action of internal machinery, like the index on the face of a clock. Whilst now it is the gymnastics of the understanding, it is hiving in the foresight of the spirit, experience in profounder laws.

The whole character and fortune of the individual are affected by the least inequalities in the culture of the understanding; for example, in the perception of differences. Therefore is Space, and therefore Time, that man may know that things are not huddled and lumped, but sundered and individual. A bell and a plough have each their use, and neither can do the office of the other. Water is good to drink, coal to burn, wool to wear; but wool cannot be drunk, nor water spun, nor coal eaten. The wise man shows his wisdom in separation, in gradation, and his scale of creatures and of merits is as wide as nature. The foolish have no range in their scale, but suppose every man is as every other man. What is not good they call the worst, and what is not hateful, they call the best.

In like manner, what good heed, nature forms in us! She pardons no mistakes. Her yea is yea, and her nay, nay.

The first steps in Agriculture, Astronomy, Zoology, (those first steps which the farmer, the hunter, and the sailor take,) teach that nature's dice are always loaded; that in her heaps and rubbish are concealed sure and useful results.

How calmly and genially the mind apprehends one after another the laws of physics! What noble emotions dilate the mortal as he enters into the counsels of the creation, and feels by knowledge the privilege to BE! His insight refines him. The beauty of nature shines in his own breast. Man is greater that he can see this, and the universe less, because Time and Space relations vanish as laws are known.

Here again we are impressed and even daunted by the immense Universe to be explored. "What we know, is a point to what we do not know." Open any recent journal of science, and weigh the problems suggested concerning Light, Heat, Electricity, Magnetism, Physiology, Geology, and judge whether the interest of natural science is likely to be soon exhausted.

Passing by many particulars of the discipline of nature, we must not omit to specify two.

THE EXERCISE OF WILL

The exercise of the Will or the lesson of power is taught in every event. From the child's successive possession of his several senses up to the hour when he saith, "Thy will be done!" he is learning the secret, that he can reduce under his will, not only particular events, but great classes, nay the whole series of events, and so conform all facts to his character. Nature is thoroughly mediate. It is made to serve. It receives the dominion of man as meekly as the ass on which the Saviour rode. It offers all its kingdoms to man as the raw material which he may mould into what is useful. Man is never weary of working it up. He forges the subtile and delicate air into wise and melodious words, and gives them wing as angels of persuasion and command. One after another, his victorious thought comes up with and reduces all things, until the world becomes, at last, only a realized will,—the double of the man.

2. Sensible objects conform to the premonitions of Reason and reflect the conscience. All things are moral; and in their boundless changes have an unceasing reference to spiritual nature. Therefore is nature glorious with form, color, and motion, that every globe in the remotest heaven; every chemical change from the rudest crystal up to the laws of life; every change of vegetation from the first principle of growth in the eye of a leaf, to the tropical forest and antediluvian coal-mine; every animal function from the sponge up to Hercules, shall hint or thunder to man the laws of right and wrong, and echo the Ten Commandments. Therefore is nature ever the ally of Religion: lends all her pomp and riches to the religious sentiment. Prophet and priest, David, Isaiah, Jesus, have drawn deeply from this source. This ethical character so penetrates the bone and marrow of nature, as to seem the end for which it was made. Whatever private purpose is answered by any member or part, this is its public and universal function, and is never omitted. Nothing in nature is exhausted in its first use. When a thing has served an end to the uttermost, it is wholly new for an ulterior service. In God, every end is converted into a new means. Thus the use of commodity, regarded by itself, is mean and squalid. But it is to the mind an education in the doctrine of Use, namely, that a thing is good only so far as it serves; that a conspiring of parts and efforts to the production of an end, is essential to any being. The first and gross manifestation of this truth, is our inevitable and hated training in values and wants, in corn and meat.

It has already been illustrated, that every natural process is a version of a moral sentence. The moral law lies at the centre of nature and radiates to the circumference. It is the pith and marrow of every substance, every relation, and every process. All things with which we deal, preach to us. What is a farm but a mute gospel? The chaff and the wheat, weeds and plants, blight, rain, insects, sun,—it is a sacred emblem from the first furrow of spring to the last stack which the snow of winter overtakes in the fields. But the sailor, the shepherd, the miner, the merchant, in their several resorts, have each an experience precisely parallel, and leading to the same conclusion: because all organizations are radically alike. Nor can it be doubted that this moral sentiment which thus scents the air, grows in the grain, and impregnates the waters of the world, is caught by man and sinks into his soul. The moral influence of nature upon every individual is that amount of truth which it illustrates to him. Who can estimate this? Who can guess how much firmness the sea-beaten rock has taught the fisherman? how much tranquillity has been reflected to man from the azure sky, over whose unspotted deeps the winds forevermore drive flocks of stormy clouds, and leave no wrinkle or stain? how much industry and providence and affection we have caught from the pantomime of brutes? What a searching preacher of self-command is the varying phenomenon of Health!

THE UNITY OF NATURE

Herein is especially apprehended the unity of Nature,—the unity in variety,—which meets us everywhere. All the endless variety of things make an identical impression. Xenophanes complained in his old age, that, look where he would, all things hastened back to Unity. He was weary of seeing the same entity in the tedious variety of forms. The fable of Proteus has a cordial truth. A leaf, a drop, a crystal, a moment of time is related to the whole, and partakes of the perfection of the whole. Each particle is a microcosm, and faithfully renders the likeness of the world....

In inquiries respecting the laws of the world and the frame of things, the highest reason is always the truest. That which seems faintly possible—it is so refined, is often faint and dim because it is deepest seated in the mind among the eternal verities. Empirical science is apt to cloud the sight, and, by the very knowledge of functions and processes, to bereave the student of the manly contemplation of the whole. The savant becomes unpoetic. But the best read naturalist who lends an entire and devout attention to truth, will see that there remains much to learn of his relation to the world, and that it is not to be learned by any addition or subtraction or other comparison of known quantities, but is arrived at by untaught sallies of the spirit, by a continual self-recovery, and by entire humility. He will perceive that there are far more excellent qualities in the student than preciseness and infallibility; that a guess is often more fruitful than an indisputable affirmation, and that a dream may let us deeper into the secret of nature than a hundred concerted experiments.

For, the problems to be solved are precisely those which the physiologist and the naturalist omit to state. It is not so pertinent to man to know all the individuals of the animal kingdom, as it is to know whence and whereto is this tyrannizing unity in his constitution, which evermore separates and classifies things, endeavoring to reduce the most diverse to one form. When I behold a rich landscape, it is less to my purpose to recite correctly the order and superposition of the strata, than to know why all thought of multitude is lost in a tranquil sense of unity. I cannot greatly honor minuteness in details, so long as there is no hint to explain the relation between things and thoughts; no ray upon the metaphysics of conchology, of botany, of the arts, to show the relation of the forms of flowers, shells, animals, architecture, to the mind, and build science upon ideas. In a cabinet of natural history, we become sensible of a certain occult recognition and sympathy in regard to the most unwieldly and eccentric forms of beast, fish, and insect. The American who has been confined, in his own country, to the sight of buildings designed after foreign models, is surprised on entering York Minster or St. Peter's at Rome, by the feeling that these structures are imitations also,—faint copies of an invisible archetype. Nor has science sufficient humanity, so long as the naturalist overlooks that wonderful congruity which subsists between man and the world; of which he is lord, not because he is the most subtile inhabitant, but because he is its head and heart, and finds something of himself in every great and small thing, in every mountain stratum, in every new law of color, fact of astronomy, or atmospheric influence which observation or analysis lay open. A perception of this mystery inspires the muse of George Herbert, the beautiful psalmist of the seventeenth century. The following lines are part of his little poem on Man.

"Man is all symmetry,
Full of proportions, one limb to another,
And to all the world besides.
Each part may call the farthest, brother;
For head with foot hath private amity,
And both with moons and tides.

"Nothing hath got so far
But man hath caught and kept it as his prey;
His eyes dismount the highest star;
He is in little all the sphere.
Herbs gladly cure our flesh, because that they
Find their acquaintance there.

"For us, the winds do blow,
The earth doth rest, heaven move, and fountains flow;
Nothing we see, but means our good,
As our delight, or as our treasure;
The whole is either our cupboard of food,
Or cabinet of pleasure.

"The stars have us to bed:
Night draws the curtain; which the sun withdraws.
Music and light attend our head.
All things unto our flesh are kind,
In their descent and being; to our mind,
In their ascent and cause.

"More servants wait on man
Than he'll take notice of. In every path,
He treads down that which doth befriend him
When sickness makes him pale and wan.
Oh mighty love! Man is one world, and hath
Another to attend him."

The perception of this class of truths makes the attraction which draws men to science, but the end is lost sight of in attention to the means. In view of this half-sight of science, we accept the sentence of Plato, that, "poetry comes nearer to vital truth than history." Every surmise and vaticination of the mind is entitled to a certain respect, and we learn to prefer imperfect theories, and sentences, which contain glimpses of truth, to digested systems which have no one valuable suggestion. A wise writer will feel that the ends of study and composition are best answered by announcing undiscovered regions of thought, and so communicating, through hope, new activity to the torpid spirit.

I shall therefore conclude this essay with some traditions of man and nature, which a certain poet sang to me; and which, as they have always been in the world, and perhaps reappear to every bard, may be both history and prophecy.

'The foundations of man are not in matter, but in spirit. But the element of spirit is eternity. To it, therefore, the longest series of events, the oldest chronologies are young and recent. In the cycle of the universal man, from whom the known individuals proceed, centuries are points, and all history is but the epoch of one degradation.

WE DISTRUST OUR SYMPATHY WITH NATURE

'We distrust and deny inwardly our sympathy with nature. We own and disown our relation to it, by turns. We are, like Nebuchadnezzar, dethroned, bereft of reason, and eating grass like an ox. But who can set limits to the remedial force of spirit?

'A man is a god in ruins. When men are innocent, life shall be longer, and shall pass into the immortal, as gently as we awake from dreams. Now, the world would be insane and rabid, if these disorganizations should last for hundreds of years. It is kept in check by death and infancy. Infancy is the perpetual Messiah, which comes into the arms of fallen men, and pleads with them to return to paradise.

'Man is the dwarf of himself. Once he was permeated and

dissolved by spirit. He filled nature with his overflowing currents. Out from him sprang the sun and moon; from man, the sun; from woman, the moon. The laws of his mind, the periods of his actions externized themselves into day and night, into the year and the seasons. But, having made for himself this huge shell, his waters retired; he no longer fills the veins and veinlets; he is shrunk to a drop. He sees, that the structure still fits him, but fits him colossally. Say, rather, once it fitted him, now it corresponds to him from far and on high. He adores timidly his own work. Now is man the follower of the sun, and woman the follower of the moon. Yet sometimes he starts in his slumber, and wonders at himself and his house, and muses strangely at the resemblance betwixt him and it. He perceives that if his law is still paramount, if still he have elemental power, if his word is sterling yet in nature, it is not conscious power, it is not inferior but superior to his will. It is Instinct.' Thus my Orphic poet sang.

At present, man applies to nature but half his force. He works on the world with his understanding alone. He lives in it, and masters it by a penny-wisdom; and he that works most in it, is but a half-man, and whilst his arms are strong and his digestion good, his mind is imbruted, and he is a selfish savage. His relation to nature, his power over it, is through the understanding; as by manure; the economic use of fire, wind, water, and the mariner's needle; steam, coal, chemical agriculture; the repairs of the human body by the dentist and the surgeon. This is such a resumption of power, as if a banished king should buy his territories inch by inch, instead of vaulting at once into his throne. Meantime, in the thick darkness, there are not wanting gleams of a better light,—occasional examples of the action of man upon nature with his entire force,—with reason as well as understanding. Such examples are; the traditions of miracles in the earliest antiquity of all nations; the history of Jesus Christ; the achievements of a principle, as in religious and political revolutions, and in the abolition of the Slave-trade; the miracles of enthusiasm, as those reported of Swedenborg, Hohenlohe, and the Shakers; many obscure and yet contested facts, now arranged under the name of Animal Magnetism; prayer; eloquence; self-healing; and the wisdom of children. These are examples of Reason's momentary grasp of the sceptre; the exertions of a power which exists not in time or space, but an instantaneous in-streaming causing power. The difference between the actual and the ideal force of man is happily figured by the schoolmen, in saying, that the knowledge of man is an evening knowledge, vespertina cognitio, but that of God is a morning knowledge, matutina cognitio.

The problem of restoring to the world original and eternal beauty, is solved by the redemption of the soul. The ruin or the blank, that we see when we look at nature, is in our own eye. The axis of vision is not coincident with the axis of things, and so they appear not transparent but opake. The reason why the world lacks unity, and lies broken and in heaps, is, because man is disunited with himself. He cannot be a naturalist, until he satisfies all the demands of the spirit. Love is as much its demand, as perception. Indeed, neither can be perfect without the other. In the uttermost meaning of the words, thought is devout, and devotion is thought. Deep calls unto deep. But in actual life, the marriage is not celebrated. There are innocent men who worship God after the tradition of their fathers, but their sense of duty has not yet extended to the use of all their faculties. And there are patient naturalists, but they freeze their subject under the wintry light of the understanding. Is not prayer also a study of truth,—a sally of the soul into the unfound infinite? No man ever prayed heartily, without learning something. But when a faithful thinker, resolute to detach every object from personal relations, and see it in the light of thought, shall, at the same time, kindle science with the fire of the holiest affections, then will God go forth anew into the creation.

THE MARK OF WISDOM

It will not need, when the mind is prepared for study, to search for objects. The invariable mark of wisdom is to see the miraculous in the common. What is a day? What is a year? What is summer? What is woman? What is a child? What is sleep? To our blindness, these things seem unaffecting. We make fables to hide the baldness of the fact and conform it, as we say, to the higher law of the mind. But when the fact is seen under the light of an idea, the gaudy fable fades and shrivels. We behold the real higher law. To the wise, therefore, a fact is true poetry, and the most beautiful of fables. These wonders are brought to our own door. You also are a man. Man and woman, and their social life, poverty, labor, sleep, fear, fortune, are known to you. Learn that none of these things is superficial, but that each phenomenon has its roots in the faculties and affections of the mind. Whilst the abstract question occupies your intellect, nature brings it in the concrete to be solved by your hands. It were a wise inquiry for the closet, to compare, point by point, especially at remarkable crises in life, our daily history, with the rise and progress of ideas in the mind.

So shall we come to look at the world with new eyes. It shall answer the endless inquiry of the intellect,—What is truth? and of the affections,—What is good? by yielding itself passive to the educated Will. Then shall come to pass what my poet said; 'Nature is not fixed but fluid. Spirit alters, moulds, makes it. The immobility or bruteness of nature, is the absence of spirit; to pure spirit, it is fluid, it is volatile, it is obedient. Every spirit builds itself a house; and beyond its house a world; and beyond its world, a heaven. Know then, that the world exists for you. For you is the phenomenon perfect. What we are, that only can we see. All that Adam had, all that Caesar could, you have and can do. Adam called his house, heaven and earth; Caesar called his house, Rome; you perhaps call yours, a cobler's trade; a hundred acres of ploughed land; or a scholar's garret. Yet line for line and point for point, your dominion is as great as theirs, though without fine names. Build, therefore, your own world. As fast as you conform your life to the pure idea in your mind, that will unfold its great proportions. A correspondent revolution in things will attend the influx of the spirit. So fast will disagreeable appearances, swine, spiders, snakes, pests, madhouses, prisons, enemies, vanish; they are temporary and shall be no more seen. The sordor and filths of na-

Humanity Should Emulate Ancient Societies' Attitude Toward Nature

KIRKPATRICK SALE

Kirkpatrick Sale, a writer and staff member of the E.F. Schumacher Society, contends that ancient peoples around the world, including Native American tribes, had a deep reverence for nature. Even though these peoples hunted animals and modified their environments, they believed that they were themselves part of their environment. Sale goes on to suggest that as recently as four hundred years ago, human beings saw themselves as occupying a world where natural phenomena such as fire, wind, and flowing water were part of a larger, living organism. Eventually, however, humans began to see themselves as apart from the natural environment, leading to an attitude that nature existed for humans to exploit.

In the beginning, as the Greeks saw it, when chaos settled into form there was a mighty sphere, floating free within the moist, gleaming embrace of the sky and its great swirling drifts of white cloud, a vibrant globe of green and blue and brown and gray, binding together in a holy, deep-breasted synchrony the temperatures of the sun, the gasses of the air, the chemicals of the sea, the minerals of the soil, and bearing the organized, self-contained, and almost purposeful aspect of a single organism, *alive,* a breathing, pulsing body that was, in the awed words of Plato, "a living creature, one and visible, containing within itself all living creatures."

To this the Greeks gave a name: Gaea, the earth mother. She was the mother of the heavens, Uranus, and of time, Cronus; of the Titans and the Cyclops; of the Meliae, the ash-tree spirits who were the progenitors of all humankind; the mother of all, first of the cosmos, creator of the creators. She became the symbol of all that was sacred and the source of all that was wise, and at the fissures and rifts in her surface—at Delphi, especially, and at Olympia and Dodona—she would impart her knowledge to those few mortals, the oracles, who knew how to hear it. . . .

EARLY SOCIETIES

The wisdom of the Greeks was not theirs alone. In fact, among the earliest societies it appears with such regularity across every continent, no matter what the climate or geography, and in every preliterate culture, that we may fairly think of it as a basic, almost innate, human perception. In virtually every hunter-gatherer society that archeologists have discovered from the paleolithic past, in almost every rudimentary society that anthropologists have studied in recent centuries, one of the central deities—in many cases the primary god, worshipped before all others—was the earth.

There is no special mystery to it. In societies whose very existence depended upon knowing the earth and how to hunt its animals and forage for its foods—the way of life for 99 percent of human history—respect for the natural world and an appreciation of the land itself as sacred and inviolable was surely inevitable. That sensibility was literally so vital that it was embedded in some central place in each culture's myths and traditions and was embodied in each culture's supreme spirits and deities.

For these early human peoples, the world around and all its features—rivers, trees, clouds, springs, mountains—were regarded as alive, endowed with spirit and sensibility every bit as real as those of humans, and in fact of exactly the same type and quality as a human's: among the Iroquois this was called *orenda,* the invisible force inherent in all parts of the universe, and in certain Bantu languages the same presence is known as *mata*.

Animals had souls, of course, so in all hunting societies some form of ritual apology and forgiveness was necessary before the kill: hence the Navajo praying to the deer before the hunt, the Mbuti cleansing themselves by smoke each morning, the Naskapi pledging to the hunted, "You and I have the same mind and spirit." But plants and flowers and trees had spirits, too, every bit as sensate, so almost all early peoples had elaborate ceremonies connected with cutting and harvesting, asking exoneration for the painful removal of some of Mother Earth's children, and most had stories like the Ojibways', which speak of "the wailing of the trees under the axe," or like the ancient Chinese tales which mention cries of "pain and indignation" from fallen branches. Hence the well-nigh universal phenomenon that anthropologists, until recently, liked to dismiss as "tree-worshipping": treating certain local trees, or groves, or whole forests as especially sacred and sacrosanct, in innate recognition of the fundamental, life-sustaining function of arboreal life on earth. From the Celts in the West to the Yalta tribes in the East, and from the Finns in the North to the Greeks in the South, trees and forests occupied a special place of spiritual honor throughout ancient Europe. Indeed among northern German tribes the Teutonic word for *temple* actually meant forest, and in Greek the word *neos,* a holy sanctuary, implied not a human-built but a natural enclosure.

Among such nature-based peoples there was no separation of the self from the world such as we have come to learn, no division between the human (willed, thinking, superior) and the non-human (conditioned, insensate, inferior). Much of the world was highly mysterious, to be sure, and many phenomena were unexplainable, but there was at the same time a liberating, psychically healthy sense of wholeness, of oneness, of place. As anthropologist Jack Forbes has said about the early California Indian tribes:

> They perceived themselves as being deeply bound together with other people (and with the surrounding non-human forms of life) in a complex interconnected web of life, that

is to say, a true community. . . . All creatures and all things were . . . brothers and sisters. From this idea came the basic principle of non-exploitation, of respect and reverence for all creatures.

Indicative of this bond is that for most of these societies the identity with the earth was so strong that their legends about creation commonly told of humanity itself emerging from a hole in the ground, or a cleft in the rocks, or the depths of a tree: the Mbuti in the Congolese rainforest, for example, say the very first human emerged from the inside of a mahogany tree, the Pueblo Indians that people climbed out of the "womb of the earth."

As a matter of fact we retain this identity in our languages today, though we, alas, no longer appreciate the association: the Indo-European word for earth, *dhghem,* is the root of the Latin *humanus,* the Old German *guman,* and the Old English *guman,* all of which meant "human." The only remnant of this sensibility I can think of today in our everyday language is *humus,* the rich, organic soil in which things grow best, though we no longer make the same connections the Latins did when we use the word.

It is natural but significant nonetheless that the deity of the earth in many societies was a woman, for the fecundity of both would be immediately obvious to any established society. This would be particularly true where, as was common until recently, the role of paternity was quite unknown and the woman's ability to give birth was as astonishing and wonderful—and necessary—as the earth's ability to regenerate itself in spring.

For the peoples of the Mediterranean and the Near East—as for the early Greeks—the Earth Goddess was at the center of spiritual constructs. Figures of "the mother goddess" are found in sacred shrines dating as far back as the Aurignacian cultures of 25,000 BC; excavations of Jarmo (6800 BC), Catal Hayuk (6500 BC), Halaf (5000 BC), Ur (4000 BC), and Elam (3000 BC) all indicate that female goddesses, and probably female priests as well, were dominant in their early religions. In

Sumeria the goddess Nammu was "the mother who gave birth to heaven and earth"; in Egypt Isis was the "oldest of the old ... from whom all becoming arose"; in Turkey the goddess Arinna was worshipped above all others, and "no other deity is as honored or great"; in Babylon Ishatar was the Queen of Heaven, "goddess of the universe [who] out of chaos brought us harmony." She was Cybele in Phrygia, Astarte in Phoenicia, Ashtoreth to the Hebrews, Athar in Syria. And her direct counterparts are found among the Irish, the Innuit Eskimos, the Japanese, the Iroquois, the Finns, the Khasis of India, the Lepcha of Sikkim, the Tallensi of West Africa. . . .

A POWERFUL TRADITION

So powerful was this Gaean tradition, so rooted in what seems to have been more than twenty millennia of religious culture, that even the male-god Indo-Europeans who invaded the Mediterranean world in about 4500 BC and successfully imposed their values on many cultures in their path could not displace it. Male deities were introduced with apparently greater frequency after this period—the Greek pantheon shifted, to take but one example, and Zeus, Adonis, and the like began appearing from about 2000 BC—but at no time were the female deities entirely supplanted, even among the ancient Hebrews. It was not until fairly late on that Judaism, then Christianity, and then Islam finally succeeded in effectively purging most forms of goddess worship from the religious cultures of the area.

Even then, however, even with the triumph of male monotheism throughout most of the Mediterranean and European worlds, even with the displacement of earth-worship for various abstract kinds of sky-worship, and even with the placement of the human (male) above all other creatures of the world—*even then* the notion of an animate earth did not completely die, certainly not among the general mass of people, religious believers or not. For all but a few, no matter what the culture or god, the world and its parts still were regarded as endowed with life and spirit and purpose, sometimes knowable to humans, or discernible, more often not. Rivers and waves and clouds and winds, obviously, were living, and trees and flowers and grasses, and fire and lightning and rain and snow—these all could be seen to move, after all—but also stones and clods of earth and mountains. In the words of historian Morris Berman:

> The view of nature which predominated in the West down to the eve of the Scientific Revolution was that of an enchanted world. Rocks, trees, rivers, and clouds were all seen as wondrous, alive, and human beings felt at home in this environment. The cosmos, in short, was a place of *belonging*. A member of this cosmos was not an alienated observer of it but a direct participant in its drama. His personal destiny was bound up with its destiny, and this relationship gave meaning to his life.

In all the long stretch of human history, it seems, from our very beginnings as tribal beings 30,000 years ago right down through classical and medieval times, until sometime in the last 400 years, the people of this planet saw themselves as inhabitants within a world alive. . . .

As benevolent as she is, however, Gaea is capable of revenge.

The Mycenaean civilization that flourished on the Aegean islands and coasts in the second millennium before Christ, say from 1600 to 1000 BC, inspired the Homeric stories, those legends of great cities and heroic dynasties, and even they failed to do justice to the complexity and grandeur of that early culture. . . .

It was a sophisticated society, with written records and a developed economy—something like a hundred different agricultural and industrial occupations were listed in the Mycenaean records—and one that sustained a prosperous system of trade and a ruling stratum with elaborate buildings, extensive land and cattle holdings, and art and artifacts of considerable richness.

It seems that the Mycenaeans were not Greeks, strictly speaking, but they clearly adopted the Greek concept of the

Earth Mother, Gaea, and sustained the elaborate Greek celebrations of her wisdom, creativity, sexuality, and fecundity; surviving artifacts show that Mycenaean shrines, probably the responsibility of a priestess caste, honored the generosity, the majesty, and the unpredictability of the goddess, her soil, her foods, her waters.

Yet somewhere, somehow, the poisons crept in. It might have been from *without*, from the so-called Dorians (probably the male-god Indo-Europeans) from the steppes of Europe, who, as art historian Vincent Scully puts it, suppressed "the old concept of the dominance of the goddess of the earth herself, seizing the sovereign power by virtue of their own thunder-wielding sky god, Zeus:" and destroyed "the old, simple, almost vegetable unity between man and nature." Or it might have come from *within*, from the decadence and carelessness, the sheer hubris of cultures that in their latter days grow too large and distended (like the Egyptians, the Persians, the Romans, the Spanish, the Toltecs, and the modern Americans, among many), for it is then that they become more concerned with exploitation and domination than nurturance and sustainability, with the riches of ores rather than the riches of the soil, with preserving bureaucracy and hierarchy rather than ecosystems and habitats.

FORGOTTEN LESSONS

Whatever the reason, the ways of Gaea were forgotten. Over the years the Mycenaeans systematically cut down the holly, cypress, olive, pine, and sycamore trees that originally covered the Mediterranean slopes, using the wood for fuel and lumber—and often as much for export, and empty riches, as for themselves. The deforested hills, unreplenished, collapsed, their topsoils and minerals washed away in the torrential Mediterranean rains, and great gouges eroded into once-fertile hillsides. Herding of goats, cattle, and swine as well as sheep became a common practice, quite heedless of the multiple effects on the countryside. It wasn't bad enough that the animals' hooves destroyed groundcover and compacted the soils, and that their teeth devoured leaves and twigs in addition to grasses, but the herders even took to setting fire to the forests to open up more areas for their flocks.

The devastation was swift and thorough, indelibly fresh in Plato's mind even seven or eight centuries later: "What now remains compared with what then existed," he wrote, "is like the skeleton of a sick man, all the fat and soft earth having been wasted away, and only the bare framework of the land being left."

And thus descended the Greek Dark Ages. The Mycenaean culture collapsed, apparently within the astonishingly short period of two generations. For the next 500 years—a considerable stretch of time, equal to the one that separates us from Columbus—Greece suffered the consequences of its heedless rapaciousness. . . .

The Mycenaean Greeks were not the only ones through history who, having abandoned the worship and having forgotten the lessons of Gaea, were taught to their dismay the hard lessons of ecological hubris. Later on the Romans, whose cumulative assaults on the Mediterranean ecology were almost certainly a central factor in the collapse of their empire—and the Sumerians, the Harappans, the Mayans, the Chinese of at least the Tang and Han dynasties, and numerous other imperial peoples who matched their dominance of humans with their dominance of nature, were forced to learn these inescapable truths.

But in no previous society did the abandonment of Gaea reach the scale it reached in Europe in the centuries after the Renaissance, the period of which we today are the exuberant consummation. For with the development of that branch of learning which usurped the word "science"—in the classical world it meant knowledge of all kinds, in the European world it was reserved for the study of a separate thing called "the natural world"—and which has dominated most intellectual and social life since the 16th century virtually all animistic, all venerative, all religious conceptions of the earth were deposed. In their stead came a new vision supported by the incontrovertible findings of physics, chemistry, mechanics, astronomy, and mathematics: the scientific worldview.

The new perception held—better than that, it *proved*—that the earth, the universe beyond it, and all within it operated according to certain clear, calculable, and unchanging laws, not by the whims of any living, sentient being. It showed that these laws were, far from being divinely created or spiritually inspired, capable of mundane scientific measurement, prediction, and replication, even scientific manipulation and control. It demonstrated that the objects of the universe, from the smallest stone to the earth's orb itself and the planets beyond, were not animate or purposeful, with individual souls and wills and spirits, but were nothing more than combinations of certain chemical and mechanical properties. It established beyond all doubt that there are not one but *two* worlds, the mechanical and inert one out there, made up of a random collection of insensate atoms, and the human one within, where thought and purpose and consciousness reside.

It achieved, in Schiller's matchless phrase, "*die Entgotterung der Natur*"—the "de-godding" of nature.

Bacon, Descartes, Newton, Galileo, all of the masterful minds of 16th- and 17th-century science, swept away, in only a few generations, the accumulated nonsense of the animistic past, much of which still lingered on even in the Europe of that time. To think of the cosmos as alive, to identify the dead matter of the earth with the organic spirit of human beings, was childish, barbarian, naive. If there was an image for the cosmos, it was not that of a goddess or any other being but something like what Newton spoke of as a giant clock, a Cosmick Machine, its many parts moving in an ordered, kinetic, mechanical way. As 17th-century physicist Robert Hooke put it, the scientific revolution enabled humankind "to discover all the secret workings of Nature, almost in the same manner as we do those that are the productions of Art and are manag'd by Wheels, and Engines, and Springs." And if God was allowed to play a part—for indeed these were all nominal Christians— he was given a role as little more than a clock-winder: "It seems probable to me," Newton wrote in 1730, "that God in the beginning formed matter in solid, massy, hard, impenetrable, movable particles, of such sizes and figures, and with such other properties and in such proportion to space as most conduced to the end for which He formed them."

Slowly and powerfully, with a growth both geometric and relentless, the ideas of the scientific paradigm transformed completely the attitudes of Western society toward nature and the cosmos. Nature was no longer either beautiful or scary but merely *there,* not to be worshipped or celebrated, but more often than not to be *used.* . . .

CONSEQUENCES

Is that too harsh? Take as an example Europe's treatment of the New World that opened up at the same time as the rise of science and the nation-states that nurtured it. Two continents, pristine jewels of unimagined glories, were perceived as nothing but empty spaces for unwanted populations, repositories of wanted ores, tracts of trees to fell and fields to plow, virgin territories with no other purpose but to be *worked.*

CHAPTER 2

THE PRESERVATION AND USE OF NATURE

AMERICAN
SOCIAL
MOVEMENTS

Environmentalists Begin to Emphasize Ecology

DONALD WORSTER

Donald Worster in this selection helps trace the shift from conservationism to modern environmentalism. He argues that the first stage of environmentalism emphasized economics, while the second stage emphasized holistic thinking, or ecology. One of the reasons for this shift was due to the devastating effect of the dust bowl experience in the 1930s, and the pioneering work of key midwestern scientists such as Frederic Clements. There is a state of nature that should serve as an ideal, Clements argued, one that overrides the needs of human societies. This ideal is the climax that nature will reach on its own if unimpeded.

Up to this point, the conservation movement in America had been overwhelmingly dominated by a series of uncoordinated resource-management programs, most of them set up around the turn of the century. Forests, water, soils, wildlife were all connected only by the loosest of conceptual threads. The major reason for this single-mindedness was that conservation policies usually had been founded on purely economic grounds; at whatever points resource demand exceeded supply, there sprouted a management program. But in the 1930s, largely as a direct consequence of the Dust Bowl experience, conservation began to move toward a more inclusive, coordinated, ecological perspective. A concern for synthesis and for maintaining the whole community of life in stable equilibrium with its habitat emerged. Undoubtedly this shift of outlook is also partly accounted for by the mood of the nation after the collapse of the Wall Street markets and the entire economic system—a mood that had become more communal and less individualistic. Holistic values everywhere challenged private, atomistic ways of thinking, and the atmosphere of depression also encouraged an unwonted willingness to subordinate economic criteria to broader standards of value, including ecological integrity. One of the unanticipated consequences of the sudden fall of America's economic empire, in other words, was the birth in the public consciousness of a new conservation philosophy, one more responsive to principles of scientific ecology. This new approach was evident in the report of the Great Plains Committee; in the regional planning of the Tennessee Valley Authority headed by David Lilienthal; in the writings of the wildlife expert Aldo Leopold; and in the organismic environmental philosophy of Lewis Mumford. In the space of thirty years, the newly independent science of ecology had moved from the early works of [Eugenius] Warming, [Henry] Cowles, and [Frederick] Clements to a position of considerable influence over government policy and popular values.

A circle of Midwestern scientists led this movement toward ecological conservation, for the grassland in particular. In 1932, for example, Roger Smith, president of the Kansas Academy of Science and entomologist at Kansas State Agricultural College, blamed the devastating outbreaks of insect pests and plant diseases in his state on the plowing of the sod and the concomitant disturbance of the natural community. "Man with his agriculture," Smith wrote, "has upset the age-old balance of nature in the great plains region, and a new balance has not been reached. It probably is a long way off, in fact, since man is constantly changing his agriculture." The result here was that chinch bugs, grasshoppers, and wireworms—all native to the area—had run wild when their natural checks were removed and they were given by unwitting farmers an abundance of attractive new food. By some means, Smith argued, Kansans must establish an artificial system of biological controls to restore order to their land. Then in 1935 the Oklahoma ecologist Paul Sears published a more comprehensive and widely influential critique of land-use practices entitled *Deserts on the March*. Though much of the book dealt with other continents, the consideration that most compelled Sears to produce it was unquestionably the dust storms that seemed to be turning the American West into a desolate, drifting Sahara. First with the destruction of the forests, then of the grasslands, he wrote, "the girdle of green about the inland deserts has been forced to give way and the desert itself literally allowed to expand." Sears advocated the appointment of a resident ecologist to supervise land use in each county with the aim of spreading the view that "all renewable natural resources are linked into a common pattern of relationship."

Both Smith and Sears contended that the pioneers had brought down on their heads this host of Egyptian plagues because they had not appreciated the genius of the climax community of the plains—the unique grass—buffalo biome. Naturally enough, then, they took their lead largely from Frederic Clements, and indeed, Clements' writings on dynamic ecology provided much of the scientific authority for the new ecological conservation movement. From the 1930s on, American environmentalists, lay as well as scientific, relied heavily on Clements' climax theory as a yardstick by which man's intrusions into nature could be measured. Their basic assumption was that the aim of land-use policy should be to leave the climax as undisturbed as possible—not on account of the intrinsic value of virgin wilderness, but more pragmatically because it had proved itself through millennial vicissitudes of climate to be stable, tenacious, and marvelously well adapted to its habitat. Whenever human interference was necessary—and most acknowledged that it was, unless the population dropped abruptly and mankind reverted to a hunting economy—they believed that the best course was to stick as tightly as you could to nature's model.

Two more of Clements' disciples were John Weaver and Evan Flory, both ecologists at the University of Nebraska; they too were among those scientists promoting a grassland conservation program founded on the ideal of the climax community. In 1934 they wrote:

> A thorough study of Nature's crops and Nature's way of making the most of a sometimes adverse environment is of scientific importance. It is also fundamental to an understanding of the effect of prairie upon stabilizing such factors as temperature and humidity, and its effect upon stabilizing the soil. It furnishes a basis for measuring the degree of departure of cultural environments from the one approved by Nature as best adapted to the climate and soil.

THE PRICE CIVILIZATION PAYS

Man's crops, they believed, are inherently more unstable, more susceptible to disease and extremes of weather, than nature's: this is part of the price civilization must pay for its very existence. But there is no need to pay to the point of bankruptcy or dust bowls. At the very least, they supposed, it would be useful to understand more precisely the penalties for disturbing the ecological balance, and then to question whether Americans were "properly utilizing Nature's prairie garden or exploiting it." Such a comparative study, they warned, "should be made now, before the opportunity with the destruction of the natural vegetation has forever passed."

Clements himself, in his several works on applied ecology written during the thirties, agreed wholeheartedly with these younger colleagues. As early as 1893, when he had been only twenty-three years old, it had been obvious to him that Nebraska homesteaders were committing a serious blunder in destroying the sod covering the sandhills of that state rather than preserving the natural grassland for grazing livestock. He recalled that Charles Bessey too, in the course of botanical surveys during the 1880s and 1890s, had come to understand that there were safer uses for those marginal lands than those he saw practiced. In the *Phytogeography*, published in 1898 by Clements and [Roscoe] Pound, "all the essential features of the proper ecological system for the development of the Great

Plains had been clearly discerned and set forth." And ignored. Clements and his associates had then been futile voices crying in the wilderness. Now, almost forty years later, he still maintained that the plains were in critical need of a broad regional plan of ecological land management faithful to the climax theory and the nurturing process of succession. It seemed to Clements that only an ecologist could see what special-interest land users such as the engineer, forester, farmer, and subdivider always overlooked: how man's actions in one place can ramify destructively through a whole biota, over thousands of square miles, across an entire nation. Such a program of management might well begin by searching out and protecting those relics of the pre-settlement formation that still grew free and wild in neglected corners of country cemeteries and along the railroad tracks where farmers could not plow. From these forsaken byways might come regeneration: the healing grass that could cover a multitude of wounds.

In dynamic ecology, it will be recalled, the climax or adult stage is the direct offspring of climate—and weather in the midcontinent is notoriously promiscuous. Ultimately, then, the ecologist must be as much a student of meteorology as of plants and animals. In the final analysis, "there is no basis for assuming either that the earth itself or the life upon it will ever reach final stability," Clements cautioned. But within the narrow span of human time-consciousness, vast periods of relative climatic stasis could be plotted with the aid of fossil records. By the same means, the ecologist might also be able to predict the future climate, knowledge vital to the farmer seeking to achieve a sustainable economy on the plains. The thirties drought, Clements maintained, was neither a freak event nor an omen of abrupt climatic change that would damn the plains to an eternally arid future. At least as far back as 1850, records showed a series of severe droughts in the West. Clements wanted to correlate this pattern with the sunspot cycle: in essence, whenever the sunspots subside to a minimum level, drought occurs. He admitted that this theory rested on a scanty statistical base, and climatologists are debating it still. It does seem clear that a major drought occurs every twenty years or so, whether due to sunspots or other causes. Recurring dry spells are a fact of life in the grassland, Clements warned, and man must explore every avenue of science that might aid in predicting them. Without such knowledge, no permanent settlement was possible.

SHIFTING ATTENTION

Clearly, this shift of attention from preserving the biological community in favor of adjusting to the climate, which Clements' writings in the 1930s emphasized, did undercut some of the force of climax conservation. Adaptation to cycles of drought rather than to a mature biome became Clements' dominant theme. This was undoubtedly an easier, more practicable route for farmers to follow, and for all his criticism of them, Clements' sympathies were often on the side of those homesteaders who were still determined to wrest a living from this intractable land. Clements did not altogether abandon the idea of climax preservation; he recommended that the westernmost edge of the shortgrass country be given over to the ranching industry and that millions of the most fragile acres in the Southwest and Great Basin area be set aside wholly for recreation or as wilderness. In these instances the aim would be to maintain the natural climax as much as possible, given the absence of Indians, bison, wolves, and many other elements of the original community. But these were the exceptions in Clements' environmental recommendations. He assumed—indeed had to, in view of the plowman's resolve— that farming would continue to be the central economic activity in the grasslands, and therefore that man would go on battling against ecological succession. Considered realistically, the function of the ecologist must be to show men how they might manipulate the sere to their advantage, by deflecting or retarding the successional process with greater care and expertise. In forest as well as prairie, Clements noted, "the climax dominants are not necessarily the most valuable to man." Inevitably then, to some extent and in some places, man's economy would always take precedence over nature's.

The Environment Must Be Restored and Preserved

GEORGE PERKINS MARSH

Logging, forest fires, and the extension of farmland rapidly reduced the forest areas of the United States. Some scientists observed a diminution in the flow of water and a decrease in rainfall. In this excerpt from *Man and Nature* written in the middle of the nineteenth century, George Perkins Marsh wrote that humans have a deleterious effect on nature when forests, wetlands, and other wilderness areas are not protected.

In reclaiming and reoccupying lands laid waste by human improvidence or malice, and abandoned by man, or occupied only by a nomade or thinly scattered population, the task of the pioneer settler is of a very different character. He is to become a coworker with nature in the reconstruction of the damaged fabric which the negligence or the wantonness of former lodgers has rendered untenantable. He must aid her in reclothing the mountain slopes with forests and vegetable mould, thereby restoring the fountains which she provided to water them; in checking the devastating fury of torrents, and bringing back the surface drainage to its primitive narrow channels; and in drying deadly morasses by opening the natural sluices which have been choked up, and cutting new canals for drawing off their stagnant waters. He must thus, on the one hand, create new reservoirs, and, on the other, remove mischievous accumulations of moisture, thereby equalizing and regulating the sources of atmospheric humidity and of flow-

Excerpted from *Man and Nature; or, Physical Geography as Modified by Human Action*, by George Perkins Marsh (New York: Scribner's, 1864).

ing water, both which are so essential to all vegetable growth, and, of course, to human and lower animal life.

DESTRUCTIVENESS OF MAN

Man has too long forgotten that the earth was given to him for usufruct alone, not for consumption, still less for profligate waste. Nature has provided against the absolute destruction of any of her elementary matter, the raw material of her works; the thunderbolt and the tornado, the most convulsive throes of even the volcano and the earthquake, being only phenomena of decomposion and recomposition. But she has left it within the power of man irreparably to derange the combinations of inorganic matter and of organic life, which through the night of æons she had been proportioning and balancing, to prepare the earth for his habitation, when, in the fulness of time, his Creator should call him forth to enter into its possession.

Apart from the hostile influence of man, the organic and the inorganic world are, as I have remarked, bound together by such mutual relations and adaptations as secure, if not the absolute permanence and equilibrium of both, a long continuance of the established conditions of each at any given time and place, or at least, a very slow and gradual succession of changes in those conditions. But man is everywhere a disturbing agent. Wherever he plants his foot, the harmonies of nature are turned to discords. The proportions and accommodations which insured the stability of existing arrangements are over-thrown. Indigenous vegetable and animal species are extirpated, and supplanted by others of foreign origin, spontaneous pro-duction is forbidden or restricted, and the face of the earth is either laid bare or covered with a new and reluctant growth of vegetable forms, and with alien tribes of animal life. These in-tentional changes and substitutions constitute, indeed, great rev-olutions; but vast as is their magnitude and importance, they are, as we shall see, insignificant in comparison with the contingent and unsought results which have flowed from them.

The fact that, of all organic beings, man alone is to be re-garded as essentially a destructive power, and that he wields energies to resist which, nature—that nature whom all material life and all inorganic substance obey—is wholly impotent, tends to prove that, though living in physical nature, he is not of her, that he is of more exalted parentage, and belongs to a higher order of existences than those born of her womb and submissive to her dictates.

There are, indeed, brute destroyers, beasts and birds and insects of prey—all animal life feeds upon, and, of course, destroys other life,—but this destruction is balanced by compensations. It is, in fact, the very means by which the existence of one tribe of animals or of vegetables is secured against being smothered by the encroachments of another; and the reproductive powers of species, which serve as the food of others, are always proportioned to the demand they are destined to supply. Man pursues his victims with reckless destructiveness; and, while the sacrifice of life by the lower animals is limited by the cravings of appetite, he unsparingly persecutes, even to extirpation, thousands of organic forms which he cannot consume.

The earth was not, in its natural condition, completely adapted to the use of man, but only to the sustenance of wild animals and wild vegetation. These live, multiply their kind in just proportion, and attain their perfect measure of strength and beauty, without producing or requiring any change in the natural arrangements of surface, or in each other's spontaneous tendencies, except such mutual repression of excessive increase as may prevent the extirpation of one species by the encroachments of another. In short, without man, lower animal and spontaneous vegetable life would have been constant in type, distribution, and proportion, and the physical geography of the earth would have remained undisturbed for indefinite periods, and been subject to revolution only from possible, unknown cosmical causes, or from geological action.

But man, the domestic animals that serve him, the field and garden plants the products of which supply him with food and clothing, cannot subsist and rise to the full development of their higher properties, unless brute and unconscious nature be effectually combated, and, in a great degree, vanquished by human art. Hence, a certain measure of transformation of terrestrial surface, of suppression of natural, and stimulation of artificially modified productivity becomes necessary. This measure man has unfortunately exceeded. He has felled the forests whose network of fibrous roots bound the mould to the rocky skeleton of the earth; but had he allowed here and there a belt of woodland to reproduce itself by spontaneous propagation, most of the mischiefs which his reckless destruction of the natural protection of the soil has occasioned would have been averted. He has broken up the mountain reservoirs, the percolation [seeping] of whose waters through unseen channels supplied the fountains that refreshed his cattle and fertilized his fields; but he has neglected to maintain the cisterns and the canals of irrigation which a wise antiquity had constructed to neutralize the consequences of its own imprudence. While he has torn the thin glebe [soil] which confined the light earth of extensive plains, and has destroyed the fringe of semi-aquatic plants which skirted the coast and checked the drifting of the sea sand, he has failed to prevent the spreading of the dunes by clothing them with artificially propagated vegetation. He has ruthlessly warred on all the tribes of animated nature whose spoil he could convert to his own uses, and he has not protected the birds which prey on the insects most destructive to his own harvests.

Purely untutored humanity, it is true, interferes comparatively little with the arrangements of nature, and the destructive agency of man becomes more and more energetic and unsparing as he advances in civilization, until the impoverishment, with which his exhaustion of the natural resources of the soil is threatening him, at last awakens him to the necessity of preserving what is left, if not of restoring what has been wantonly wasted. The wandering savage grows no cultivated vegetable, fells no forest, and extirpates no useful plant, no noxious weed. If his skill in the chase enables him to entrap numbers of the animals on which he feeds, he compensates this loss by destroying also the lion, the tiger, the wolf, the otter, the seal, and the eagle, thus indirectly protecting the feebler quadrupeds and fish and fowls, which would otherwise become the booty of beasts and birds of prey. But with stationary life, or rather with the pastoral state, man at once commences an almost indiscriminate warfare upon all the forms of animal and vegetable existence around him, and as he advances in civilization, he gradually eradicates or transfoms every spontaneous product of the soil he occupies.

HUMAN AND BRUTE ACTION COMPARED

It has been maintained by authorities as high as any known to modern science, that the action of man upon nature, though greater in *degree,* does not differ in *kind,* from that of wild animals. It appears to me to differ in essential character, because, though it is often followed by unforeseen and undesired results, yet it is nevertheless guided by a self-conscious and intelligent will aiming as often at secondary and remote as at immediate objects. The wild animal, on the other hand, acts instinctively, and, so far as we are able to perceive, always with a view to single and direct purposes. The backwoodsman and the beaver alike fell trees; the man that he may convert the forest into an olive grove that will mature its fruit only for a succeeding generation, the beaver that he may feed upon their bark or use them in the construction of his habitation. Human differs from brute action, too, in its influence upon the material world, because it is not controlled by natural compensations and balances. Natural arrangements, once disturbed by man, are not restored until he retires from the field, and leaves free scope to spontaneous recuperative energies; the wounds he inflicts upon the material creation are not healed until he withdraws the arm that gave the blow. On the other hand, I am not aware of any evidence that wild animals have ever destroyed the smallest forest, extirpated any organic species, or modified its natural character, occasioned any permanent change of terrestrial surface, or produced any disturbance of physical conditions which nature has not, of herself, repaired without the expulsion of the animal that had caused it.

The form of geographical surface, and very probably the climate of a given country, depend much on the character of the vegetable life belonging to it. Man has, by domestication, greatly changed the habits and properties of the plants he rears; he has, by voluntary selection, immensely modified the forms and qualities of the animated creatures that serve him; and he has, at the same time, completely rooted out many forms of both vegetable and animal being. What is there, in the influence of brute life, that corresponds to this? We have no reason to believe that in that portion of the American continent which, though peopled by many tribes of quadruped and fowl, remained uninhabited by man, or only thinly occupied by purely savage tribes, any sensible geographical change had occurred within twenty centuries before the epoch of discovery and colonization while, during the same period, man had changed millions of square miles, in the fairest and most fertile regions of the Old World, into the barrenest deserts.

The ravages committed by man subvert the relations and destroy the balance which nature had established between her organized and her inorganic creations; and she avenges herself upon the intruder, by letting loose upon her defaced provinces destructive energies hitherto kept in check by organic forces destined to be his best auxiliaries, but which he has unwisely dispersed and driven from the field of action. When the forest is gone, the great reservoir of moisture stored up in its vegetable mould is evaporated, and returns only in deluges of rain to wash away the parched dust into which that mould has been converted. The well-wooded and humid hills are turned to ridges of dry rock, which encumbers the low grounds and chokes the watercourses with its debris, and—except in countries favored with an equable distribution of rain through the seasons, and a moderate and regular inclination of surface— the whole earth, unless rescued by human art from the physical degradation to which it tends, becomes an assemblage of bald mountains, of barren, turfless hills, and of swampy and malarious plains. There are parts of Asia Minor, of Northern Africa, of Greece, and even of Alpine Europe, where the operation of causes set in action by man has brought the face of

ture, and it is unprofitable, on the other, to speculate on what may be accomplished by the discovery of now unknown and unimagined natural forces, or even by the invention of new arts and new processes. But since we have seen aerostation [lighter than air balloon], the motive power of elastic vapors, the wonders of modern telegraphy, the destructive explosiveness of gunpowder, and even of a substance so harmless, unresisting, and inert as cotton, nothing in the way of mechanical achievement seems impossible, and it is hard to restrain the imagination from wandering forward a couple of generations to an epoch when our descendants shall have advanced as far beyond us in physical conquest, as we have marched beyond the trophies erected by our grandfathers.

I must therefore be understood to mean only, that no agencies now known to man and directed by him seem adequate to the reducing of great Alpine precipices to such slopes as would enable them to support a vegetable clothing, or to the covering of large extents of denuded rock with earth, and planting upon them a forest growth. But among the mysteries which science is yet to reveal, there may be still undiscovered methods of accomplishing even grander wonders than these. Mechanical philosophers have suggested the possibility of accumulating and treasuring up for human use some of the greater natural forces, which the action of the elements puts forth with such astonishing energy. Could we gather, and bind, and make subservient to our control, the power which a West Indian hurricane exerts through a small area in one continuous blast, or the momentum expended by the waves, in a tempestuous winter, upon the breakwater at Cherbourg, or the lifting power of the tide, for a month, at the head of the Bay of Fundy, or the pressure of a square mile of sea water at the depth of five thousand fathoms, or a moment of the might of an earthquake or a volcano, our age—which moves no mountains and casts them into the sea by faith alone—might hope to scarp the rugged walls of the Alps and Pyrenees and Mount Taurus, robe them once more in a vegetation as rich as that of their pristine woods, and turn their wasting torrents into refreshing streams.

Could this old world, which man has overthrown, be re-builded, could human cunning rescue its wasted hillsides and its deserted plains from solitude or mere nomade occupation, from barrenness, from nakedness, and from insalubrity [un-health], and restore the ancient fertility and healthfulness of the Etruscan sea coast, the Campagna and the Pontine marshes, of Calabria, of Sicily, of the Peloponnesus and insular and conti-nental Greece, of Asia Minor, of the slopes of Lebanon and Hermon, of Palestine, of the Syrian desert, of Mesopotamia and the delta of the Euphrates, of the Cyrenaica, of Africa proper, Numidia, and Mauritania, the thronging millions of Europe might still find room on the Eastern continent, and the main current of emigration be turned toward the rising instead of the setting sun.

But changes like these must await great political and moral revolutions in the governments and peoples by whom those regions are now possessed, a command of pecuniary and of mechanical means not at present enjoyed by those nations, and a more advanced and generally diffused knowledge of the processes by which the amelioration of soil and climate is pos-sible, than now anywhere exists. Until such circumstances shall conspire to favor the work of geographical regeneration, the countries I have mentioned, with here and there a local ex-ception, will continue to sink into yet deeper desolation, and in the mean time, the American continent, Southern Africa, Australia, and the smaller oceanic islands, will be almost the only theatres where man is engaged, on a great scale, in trans-forming the face of nature.

Natural Resources Must Be Conserved

THEODORE ROOSEVELT

Theodore Roosevelt, twenty-sixth president of the United States, promoted conservation and the wise use of natural resources more than any chief executive in American history. As president, Roosevelt is remembered for setting aside national forests, initiating a national wildlife refuge system, and advocating the wise use of farmland to prevent erosion. Under his administration Gifford Pinchot headed the nation's Forest Service as part of the Agriculture department. What follows is a portion of the speech Roosevelt gave to a 1907 governors' conference. There, he used the "bully pulpit" of the presidency to instill enthusiasm for conservation into a broad array of national leaders.

This Conference on the conservation of natural resources is in effect a meeting of the representatives of all the people of the United States called to consider the weightiest problem now before the Nation; and the occasion for the meeting lies in the fact that the natural resources of our country are in danger of exhaustion if we permit the old wasteful methods of exploiting them longer to continue.

GROWTH IN DEMAND

With the rise of peoples from savagery to civilization, and with the consequent growth in the extent and variety of the needs of the average man, there comes a steadily increasing growth of the amount demanded by this average man from the actual resources of the country. And yet, rather curiously, at the same time that there comes that increase in what the average man

Excerpted from the "Opening Address by the President," by Theodore Roosevelt, in *Proceedings of the Conference of Governors in the White House*, edited by Newton C. Blanchard (Washington, DC: GPO, 1909).

demands from the resources, he is apt to grow to lose the sense of his dependence upon nature. He lives in big cities. He deals in industries that do not bring him in close touch with nature. He does not realize the demands he is making upon nature. . . .

In [George] Washington's time anthracite coal was known only as a useless black stone; and the great fields of bituminous coal were undiscovered. As steam was unknown, the use of coal for power production was undreamed of. Water was practically the only source of power, save the labor of men and animals; and this power was used only in the most primitive fashion. But a few small iron deposits had been found in this country, and the use of iron by our countrymen was very small. Wood was practically the only fuel, and what lumber was sawed was consumed locally, while the forests were regarded chiefly as obstructions to settlement and cultivation. The man who cut down a tree was held to have conferred a service upon his fellows.

Such was the degree of progress to which civilized mankind had attained when this nation began its career. It is almost impossible for us in this day to realize how little our Revolutionary ancestors knew of the great store of natural resources whose discovery and use have been such vital factors in the growth and greatness of this Nation, and how little they required to take from this store in order to satisfy their needs.

Since then our knowledge and use of the resources of the present territory of the United States have increased a hundred-fold. Indeed, the growth of this Nation by leaps and bounds makes one of the most striking and important chapters in the history of the world. Its growth has been due to the rapid development, and alas that it should be said! to the rapid destruction, of our natural resources. Nature has supplied to us in the United States, and still supplies to us, more kinds of resources in a more lavish degree than has ever been the case at any other time or with any other people. Our position in the world has been attained by the extent and thoroughness of the control we have achieved over nature; but we are more, and not less, dependent upon what she furnishes than at any previous time of history since the days of primitive man.

... The wise use of all of our natural resources, which are our national resources as well, is the great material question of today. I have asked you to come together now because the enormous consumption of these resources, and the threat of imminent exhaustion of some of them, due to reckless and wasteful use, ... calls for common effort, common action.

We want to take action that will prevent the advent of a woodless age, and defer as long as possible the advent of an ironless age....

A great many of these things are truisms. Much of what I say is so familiar to us that it seems commonplace to repeat it; but familiar though it is, I do not think as a nation we understand what its real bearing is. It is so familiar that we disregard it. [Applause]

The steadily increasing drain on these natural resources has promoted to an extraordinary degree the complexity of our industrial and social life. Moreover, this unexampled development has had a determining effect upon the character and opinions of our people. The demand for efficiency in the great task has given us vigor, effectiveness, decision, and power, and a capacity for achievement which in its own lines has never yet been matched....

RESOURCES ARE BEING EXHAUSTED

[I]t is safe to say that the prosperity of our people depends directly on the energy and intelligence with which our natural resources are used. It is equally clear that these resources are the final basis of national power and perpetuity. Finally, it is ominously evident that these resources are in the course of rapid exhaustion.

This Nation began with the belief that its landed possessions were illimitable and capable of supporting all the people who might care to make our country their home; but already the limit of unsettled land is in sight, and indeed but little land fitted for agriculture now remains unoccupied save what can be reclaimed by irrigation and drainage—a subject with which this Conference is partly to deal. We began with an unapproached heritage of forests; more than half of the timber is gone. We began with coal fields more extensive than those of any other nation and with iron ores regarded as inexhaustible, and many experts now declare that the end of both iron and coal is in sight. . . .

[W]e began with soils of unexampled fertility, and we have so impoverished them by injudicious use and by failing to check erosion that their crop-producing power is diminishing instead of increasing. In a word, we have thoughtlessly, and to a large degree unnecessarily, diminished the resources upon which not only our prosperity but the prosperity of our children and our children's children must always depend.

We have become great in a material sense because of the lavish use of our resources, and we have just reason to be proud of our growth. But the time has come to inquire seriously what will happen when our forests are gone, when the coal, the iron, the oil, and the gas are exhausted, when the soils shall have been still further impoverished and washed into the streams, polluting the rivers, denuding the fields, and obstructing navigation. These questions do not relate only to the next century or to the next generation. One distinguishing characteristic of really civilized men is foresight; we have to, as a nation, exercise foresight for this nation in the future; and if we do not exercise that foresight, dark will be the future! [Applause] We should exercise foresight now, as the ordinarily prudent man exercises foresight in conserving and wisely using the property which contains the assurance of well-being for himself and his children. We want to see a man own his farm rather than rent it, because we want to see it an object to him to transfer it in better order to his children. We want to see him exercise forethought for the next generation. We need to exercise it in some fashion ourselves as a nation for the next generation.

NONRENEWABLE AND RENEWABLE RESOURCES

The natural resources I have enumerated can be divided into two sharply distinguished classes accordingly as they are or are not capable of renewal. Mines if used must necessarily be exhausted. The minerals do not and can not renew themselves. Therefore in dealing with the coal, the oil, the gas, the iron, the metals generally, all that we can do is to try to see that they are wisely used. The exhaustion is certain to come in time. We can trust that it will be deferred long enough to enable the extraordinarily inventive genius of our people to devise means and methods for more or less adequately replacing what is lost; but the exhaustion is sure to come.

The second class of resources consists of those which can not only be used in such manner as to leave them undiminished for our children, but can actually be improved by wise use. The soil, the forests, the waterways come in this category. Every one

Theodore Roosevelt

knows that a really good farmer leaves his farm more valuable at the end of his life than it was when he first took hold of it. So with the waterways. So with the forests. In dealing with mineral resources, man is able to improve on nature only by putting the resources to a beneficial use which in the end exhausts them; but in dealing with the soil and its products man can improve on nature by compelling the resources to renew and even reconstruct themselves in such manner as to serve increasingly beneficial uses—while the living waters can be so controlled as to multiply their benefits.

Neither the primitive man nor the pioneer was aware of any duty to posterity in dealing with the renewable resources. When the American settler felled the forests, he felt that there was plenty of forest left for the sons who came after him. When he exhausted the soil of his farm, he felt that his son could go West and take up another. The Kentuckian or the Ohioan felled the forest and expected his son to move west and fell other forests on the banks of the Mississippi; the Georgian exhausted his farm and moved into Alabama or to the mouth of the Yazoo to take another. So it was with his immediate successors. When the soil-wash from the farmer's field choked the neighboring river, the only thought was to use the railway rather than the boats to move produce and supplies. That was so up to the generation that preceded ours.

Now all this is changed. On the average the son of the farmer of today must make his living on his father's farm. There is no difficulty in doing this if the father will exercise wisdom. No wise use of a farm exhausts its fertility. So with the forests. We are over the verge of a timber famine in this country, and it is unpardonable for the Nation or the States to permit any further cutting of our timber save in accordance with a system which will provide that the next generation shall see the timber increased instead of diminished. [Applause]

Just let me interject one word as to a particular type of folly of which it ought not to be necessary to speak. We stop wasteful cutting of timber; that of course makes a slight shortage at the moment. To avoid that slight shortage at the moment, there are certain people so foolish that they will incur absolute shortage in the future, and they are willing to stop all attempts to conserve the forests, because of course by wastefully using them at the moment we can for a year or two provide against any lack of wood. That is like providing for the farmer's family to live sumptuously on the flesh of the milch cow. [Laughter] Any farmer can live pretty well for a year if he is content not to live at all the year after. [Laughter and applause] . . .

We are coming to recognize as never before the right of the Nation to guard its own future in the essential matter of natural resources. In the past we have admitted the right of the individual to injure the future of the Republic for his own present profit. In fact there has been a good deal of a demand for unrestricted individualism, for the right of the individual to injure the future of all of us for his own temporary and immediate profit. The time has come for a change. As a people we have the right and the duty, second to none other but the

right and duty of obeying the moral law, of requiring and doing justice, to protect ourselves and our children against the
wasteful development of our natural resources, whether that
waste is caused by the actual destruction of such resources or
by making them impossible of development hereafter. . . .

Finally, let us remember that the conservation of our natural resources, though the gravest problem of today, is yet but
part of another and greater problem to which this Nation is
not yet awake, but to which it will awake in time, and with
which it must hereafter grapple if it is to live—the problem of
national efficiency, the patriotic duty of insuring the safety and
continuance of the Nation. [Applause] When the People of
the United States consciously undertake to raise themselves as
citizens, and the Nation and the States in their several spheres,
to the highest pitch of excellence in private, State, and national
life, and to do this because it is the first of all the duties of true
patriotism, then and not till then the future of this Nation, in
quality and in time, will be assured.

The Federal Government's Role in Land Conservation Expands

William G. Robbins

In this selection forestry historian William G. Robbins discusses the beginning of a new era in American environmentalism, the conservation movement. Robbins traces the history of key pieces of legislation that transferred control of the nation's forest reserves from the U.S. Department of the Interior to the U.S. Department of Agriculture. These bureaucratic and legislative changes resulted in the nation's forests being professionally and scientifically managed for the first time.

The appointment of the energetic Gifford Pinchot to head the Division of Forestry in 1898 marks the beginning of a new era in federal policy. The changes that took place during Pinchot's tenure have shaped the administration and jurisdiction of federal forestry ever since. In 1898 Pinchot headed a small staff without a forest to manage. Three years later Congress advanced the Division of Forestry to bureau status, thus strengthening the agency's position and giving it more prestige in the Department of Agriculture. Then in 1905, the most significant move of all—the transfer of 63 million acres of federal forestland to the Department of Agriculture. In recognition of its new status, the bureau was renamed the Forest Service (July, 1905), and two years later the federal timberlands were designated as national forests. These expanded responsi-

Excerpted from *American Forestry: A History of National, State, and Private Cooperation,* by William G. Robbins. Copyright © 1985 by the University of Nebraska Press. Reprinted by permission of the University of Nebraska Press.

bilities entailed a dramatic increase in staff—from eleven employees in 1898 to 821 in 1905. The modern Forest Service bureaucracy was born.

Pinchot is an intimate part of federal forestry. Born to wealth and comfortable living and amidst a family overly solicitous for his welfare, Pinchot established a reputation for spartan energy and hard work. He was more than six feet tall, slim, and sported a thick moustache (the latter a delight to cartoonists). Despite a sheltered upbringing, the Yale graduate was a man of strong personality who attracted great loyalty from his supporters and equally strong opposition from those who disagreed with him. William B. Greeley, whose influence on the Forest Service ranks second to that of Pinchot, remarked that Pinchot brought to forestry "a religious intensity and a magnetic personal leadership that have rarely been equalled in the American drama." Magnanimous words about a man he often disagreed with.

CREATOR AND INSPIRATION

Pinchot both created and inspired the modern Forest Service. He established a model of efficient agency management. He demanded that subordinates respond immediately to requests and had a special fetish for answering letters on time. An independent study of the Forest Service administration in 1908 paid high tribute to Pinchot's administrative ability. "Rarely, if ever," the report concluded, have we "met a body of men where the average of intelligence was so high, or the loyalty to the organization and the work so great." The study added that the agency had conducted a volume of business "worthy of the highest commendation."

Pinchot was an avowed publicist for "practicing Forestry in the woods." He criticized the old forestry division for its failure to produce "any forest management whatsoever," and demanded that the Washington office spend time in the field observing the practical problems of bringing forestry to the woods. The potential for this work was virtually limitless— "The world was all before us," he exclaimed. "I could pick my own trail." And there was little doubt about the direction he would choose. Just as the "business" of farmers was to manage farms, the "business" of foresters would be to manage forests. It was in pursuit of these objectives that Pinchot vastly expanded and extended federal forestry cooperation with the private sector.

Only four months after his appointment, the office published Pinchot's famous Circular No. 21, which offered advice "to farmers, lumbermen, and others" in managing their forestlands. The service was free to woodlot owners, but the division charged traveling expenses and subsistence costs "in the case of large tracts." Nine months after the publication of "our major offensive," the division was "totally unable to meet the public demand upon it. " And by 1902 requests continued "to outstrip more and more the ability of the Bureau to meet them." This was the first federal program that was universally popular among timberland owners.

But Circular No. 21 was more; it was the first federal program to offer assistance in the field. Before the program was cut back in 1909, federal foresters had examined approximately 8 million acres, mostly in large holdings. These landowners included William G. Rockefeller, Abram S. Hewitt, E.H. Harriman, the St. Regis Paper Company, the Great Northern Paper Company, the Weyerhaeuser Timber Company, and the Kirby Lumber Company.

Despite the popularity of Circular No. 21, the Bureau of Forestry devoted most of its energies to government work, even before the transfer of the forest reserves to the Department of Agriculture. In 1903 Pinchot noted that "a very large proportion" of the bureau's activity involved federal lands. But the agency could neglect the needs of private holders only at the risk of "seriously endangering the object of its existence." Pinchot then outlined what was to become a central theme for increased federal assistance. In meeting private requests for aid, he observed, "it is the public rather than any private interest which is at stake." This refrain anticipated industry arguments before congressional committees in the 1920s, the appeals for increased aid to lumbermen in the 1930s, and especially the testimony calling for the expansion of federal forestry programs after the Second World War. Pinchot was a thoroughgoing modernist in recognizing the principal argument for government-industry cooperation.

The government intended Circular No. 21 assistance as a temporary arrangement to prepare the way for the private forester. J. Girvin Peters told the Society of American Foresters that the federal bureau did not intend to compete with private forestry. But because the bureau had to create a "working field," it sought cooperation with private owners and "offered very generous terms." At first the government carried three-fourths of the costs, but this share diminished as the demand for assistance increased. By 1904, Peters pointed out, owners were paying for all "the expense of the cooperation" except the salaries of bureau officials and office work. The government, he said, was making an effort to transfer every expense to the timberland owner.

But for "the holders of small parcels of land," Peters outlined a different approach. Because hiring a private forester was not practical for this class of owner, the Bureau of Forestry would continue to offer free preliminary examinations. Government aid to small holders, he concluded, "will always be a cardinal feature of the Bureau's cooperative work." The federal agency continued direct assistance to individual landowners for several years but disbanded the practice when federal legislation opened the way for greater aid through the individual states. But the most important reason for the cutback in direct cooperation with private holders was the Forest Service responsibility for managing the national forests after 1905.

Because of the broadened scope of the cooperative programs, the Pinchot administration continually struggled with policy memoranda outlining cooperative agreements. The Service Committee, a policy-making group organized in 1903 and comprised of the head forester and the division heads, debated and then drafted the administrative directives for the cooperative programs. The committee's deliberations were sometimes lengthy, and the record reveals considerable disagreement about the appropriate federal role. The committee's responsibilities were broad. It negotiated cooperation between forestry and other divisions and bureaus within the Department of Agriculture. The committee tendered a request from the Division of Agrostology for cooperation in the reclamation of sand dunes. In this instance (April 25, 1903), Pinchot advised accepting the offer "for diplomatic reasons." Such a move, he said, would leave the bureau "more at liberty to carry on its work along this line."

WORKING WITH THE INTERIOR DEPARTMENT

One of the more important cooperative relationships during the early Pinchot years was the bureau's working association with the Department of the Interior. Because Interior had jurisdiction over the federal forests, and because the foresters were in the Department of Agriculture, the two departments drafted agreements for the management of the forest reserves. For Pinchot's staff, the work load was heavy. Pinchot repeatedly mentioned the Interior Department's demands upon his staff for the preparation of "working plans" similar to those drafted for private owners. When President Theodore Roosevelt signed the transfer act into law, the management of the federal forests became a major housekeeping responsibility rather than a negotiated commitment of technical expertise.

The federal agency also continued some of the cooperative agreements initiated under Fernow [Bernhard Fernow, Pinchot's immediate predecessor, as chief forester]. Pinchot provided small sums of money for "collaborators"—persons "of established reputation in forestry" but not associated with the division—"who have knowledge of special value to it." Dispersed across the country, these "collaborators" wrote authoritative pieces "at a very moderate cost." This form of cooperation, Pinchot related in his autobiography, was an effort to gain the expertise of people with training in the sciences.

Although Pinchot's policies differed from those of his predecessor, he continued the practice of making cooperative agreements in tree planting. He replaced Fernow's practice of cooperating with state agricultural experiment stations by providing advice to tree planters similar to that offered under Circular No. 21. The cooperative tree-planting program, outlined in Circular No. 22, had its greatest impact in the Plains states. The planting program again distinguished between large and small tracts. Federal foresters provided owners of fewer than five acres with free advice and assistance, but the program did not include the expenses of planting and caring for the trees. On larger acreages the preliminary inspection was free, but landowners were responsible for all subsequent expenses.

Under Fernow's administration, the division's planting program had serious problems. When newspapers announced that the government was giving away trees, people applied for seedlings with little knowledge about proper planting techniques. To make matters worse, the government made contracts with private growers who often palmed off their unsalable inventories to the applicants. On one occasion a private supplier provided an applicant with wild stock pulled from the ground with the bare roots exposed. For these reasons the division discontinued its free distribution of seed stock and adopted the policy described in Circular No. 22.

But problems persisted. A Bureau of Forestry investigation in the summer of 1903 revealed that applicants had planted only 50 percent of the acreages agreed to. When the bureau revised and tightened the requirements, the move created even greater difficulties. George L. Clothier, a bureau assistant involved with cooperative tree planting, thought the 1903 revision bristled with "threats of charges to the landowner." The new policy, he claimed, "was made in the spirit of hostility to the landowner," as though the bureau was prepared "not to be again 'taken in' by imposters." Clothier warned that it would frighten away farmers "who never rode in sleeping cars." Despite the clearly stated offer that the Department of Agriculture still provided free preliminary examinations, the number who applied for farm planting declined. Clothier thought he knew why; it was the abuses of private nurserymen who sold farmers deficient stock. The Forest Service subsequently issued another revision of Circular No. 22 with an "entirely new outline" for planting cooperation.

By 1906 the Forest Service had extended its planting assistance to large landholders whose motives, according to Pinchot, were "purely economic." At the same time the Forest Service increased its work with the Bureau of Reclamation; most of these projects involved planting along government-financed canals in the arid West. But when Congress transferred the forest reserves to its jurisdiction, the service lost interest in tree planting. The Office of Dry Land Agriculture continued experimental planting in the Plains states with some success for the next few decades, but the Forest Service did not take up cooperative planting again until the expanded authorization under the Clarke-McNary Act of 1924.

A FOREST RESERVE

During the Pinchot years federal foresters also conducted field work with the U.S. Geological Survey (USGS), especially to gather information for the proposed Appalachian forest reserve. Pressure to establish an eastern reserve gathered momentum in 1900, when Congress authorized the forestry office and the USGS to conduct a joint study of the southern Appalachians. The exhaustive report, completed in 1901, formed the basis for the eventual establishment of national forests in the region. The annual reports also mention cooperative work with the Department of War, assessing timber sales on military reservations, and drafting working plans for the improvement of timber stands.

The federal government also expanded forestry research in the first decade of the new century. The Pinchot staff conducted field investigations of commercially valuable trees to determine their distribution and reproduction characteristics, and in 1903 Pinchot established the Section of Silvics "to contribute to ordered and scientific knowledge of our forests." At the same time the bureau cooperated with the Bureau of Entomology to study "remedies" for combating insect damage.

Although these investigations were important, there was no plan for coordinating the research findings until Raphael Zon, a Russian immigrant and graduate of Cornell, suggested the establishment of experiment stations. Zon, who visited Germany, Austria, and France in the winter of 1908, recommended separate branches for research and administrative work. The Forest Service implemented this strategy in 1915, when it created the Branch of Research. As head of the Section of Silvics, Zon was chiefly responsible for setting up the first forest experiment station on the Coconino National Forest in Arizona in 1908; and with McGarvey Cline, he established the Forest Products Laboratory at Madison, Wisconsin, in 1910.

The function of research, according to Zon, was practical—to "supply technical facts." Forestry research should solve "immediate practical problems" encountered in daily industrial activity. Through the influence of Zon and others, Forest Service research developed as an integral part of federal cooperation with the producers and users of forest products. The investigations embraced a wide array of activities—studies of lumber industry economics, market inquiries, and the compilation of statistics on lumber prices (the agency began the latter practice in 1908 with the cooperation of wholesale lumbermen).

By the time William Howard Taft dismissed Pinchot in January, 1910, the Forest Service had established the general outlines of a cooperative policy. Fernow's programs and the vastly expanded activities of the Pinchot administration both emphasized the importance of private forests to the national welfare. And both men directed their appeals to the acquisitive side of timberland ownership. Pinchot's Circular No. 21 advised owners to "understand that it pays better . . . to protect a forest, in harvesting a timber crop, than to destroy it." Thus, the government packaged its cooperative program in the form of federal advisory assistance to assure future timber supplies.

Although the Forest Service curtailed its forest management and tree-planting assistance after the transfer of the forest reserves to the Department of Agriculture, the agency became involved in several other cooperative commitments with federal bureaus and departments, colleges and universities, and, more important, with a growing number of state agencies. But Pinchot recognized a continued responsibility to the private sector when he organized the Division of State and Private Forestry in 1908. The new division immediately undertook a study of forest taxation in cooperation with individual states. Federal forestry officials also had to work out procedures for cooperating with the Reclamation Service, the USGS, the General Land Office, and the Indian Office.

ESTABLISHING A PRECEDENT

The early cooperative programs established a precedent for federal forestry. They offered federal outreach assistance to landowners, processors, and consumers of forest products and gave public visibility to Forest Service officers. The government's cooperative assistance programs also opened up employment opportunities for an increasing number of graduate foresters. As a profession with close ties to the lumber industry, forestry came of age in the first decade of the twentieth century. The groundwork for this advance, however, lay in the last thirty years of the nineteenth century when an astonishing growth in public consciousness about the importance of the forest resources took place.

But the activities of scientists and federal foresters explain only part of the development of cooperative forestry assistance. As with virtually all federal resource programs, industrial conditions determined policy. In this case, lumber industry spokesmen and their allies in the Forest Service defined and molded federal programs to meet the requirements for a modern lumber economy. That many of these individuals moved easily from public to private employment underscores the congeniality and common purpose that characterized many of the federal assistance programs.

CHAPTER 3

A NEW RELATIONSHIP WITH NATURE

Nature Is a Refuge That Must Be Preserved

JOHN MUIR

Naturalist John Muir helped persuade the American public that wilderness areas were irreplaceable treasures that must be protected from exploitation. Some consider him a central force in persuading the federal government to set aside lands as national parks. The following selection from the *Atlantic Monthly,* published in 1898, gives an idea of the poetic power and sweep of his writing that so influenced millions, including, significantly, President Theodore Roosevelt, who added millions of acres to the national forest.

The tendency nowadays to wander in wildernesses is delightful to see. Thousands of tired, nerve-shaken, over-civilized people are beginning to find out that going to the mountains is going home; that wildness is a necessity; and that mountain parks and reservations are useful not only as fountains of timber and irrigating rivers, but as fountains of life. Awakening from the stupefying effects of the vice of over-industry and the deadly apathy of luxury, they are trying as best they can to mix and enrich their own little ongoings with those of Nature, and to get rid of rust and disease. Briskly venturing and roaming, some are washing off sins and cobweb cares of the devil's spinning in all-day storms on mountains; sauntering in rosiny pinewoods or in gentian meadows, brushing through chaparral, bending down and parting sweet, flowery sprays; tracing rivers to their sources, getting in touch with the nerves of Mother Earth; jumping from rock to rock, feel-

Excerpted from "The Wild Parks and Forest Reservations of the West," by John Muir, *The Atlantic Monthly*, 1898.

ing the life of them, learning the songs of them, panting in whole-souled exercise and rejoicing in deep, long-drawn breaths of pure wildness. This is fine and natural and full of promise. And so also is the growing interest in the care and preservation of forests and wild places in general, and in the half-wild parks and gardens of towns. Even the scenery habit in its most artificial forms, mixed with spectacles, silliness, and kodaks; its devotees arrayed more gorgeously than scarlet tanagers, frightening the wild game with red umbrellas,—even this is encouraging, and may well be regarded as a hopeful sign of the times.

All the Western mountains are still rich in wildness, and by means of good roads are being brought nearer civilization every year. To the sane and free it will hardly seem necessary to cross the continent in search of wild beauty, however easy the way, for they find it in abundance wherever they chance to be. Like Thoreau they see forests in orchards and patches of huckleberry brush, and oceans in ponds and drops of dew. Few in these hot, dim, frictiony times are quite sane or free; choked with care like clocks full of dust, laboriously doing so much good and making so much money,—or so little,—they are no longer good themselves.

When, like a merchant taking a list of his goods, we take stock of our wildness, we are glad to see how much of even the most destructible kind is still unspoiled. Looking at our continent as scenery when it was all wild, lying between beautiful seas, the starry sky above it, the starry rocks beneath it, to compare its sides, the East and the West, would be like comparing the sides of a rainbow. But it is no longer equally beautiful. The rainbows of to-day are, I suppose, as bright as those that first spanned the sky; and some of our landscapes are growing more beautiful from year to year, notwithstanding the clearing, trampling work of civilization. New plants and animals are enriching woods and gardens, and many landscapes wholly new, with divine sculpture and architecture, are just now coming to the light of day as the mantling folds of creative glaciers are being withdrawn, and life in a thousand cheerful, beautiful forms is pushing into them, and new-born rivers are beginning to sing and shine in them. The old rivers, too, are growing longer like healthy trees, gaining new branches and lakes as the residual glaciers at their highest sources on the mountains recede, while their rootlike branches in the flat deltas are at the same time spreading farther and wider into the seas and making new lands.

Under the control of the vast mysterious forces of the interior of the earth all the continents and islands are slowly rising or sinking. Most of the mountains are diminishing in size under the wearing action of the weather, though a few are increasing in height and girth, especially the volcanic ones, as fresh floods of molten rocks are piled on their summits and spread in successive layers, like the wood-rings of trees, on their sides. And new mountains are being created from time to time as islands in lakes and seas, or as subordinate cones on the slopes of old ones, thus in some measure balancing the waste of old beauty with new. Man, too, is making many far-reaching changes. This most influential half animal, half angel is rapidly multiplying and spreading, covering the seas and lakes with ships, the land with huts, hotels, cathedrals, and clustered city shops and homes, so that soon, it would seem, we may have to go farther than Nansen to find a good sound solitude. None of Nature's landscapes are ugly so long as they are wild; and much, we can say comfortingly, must always be in great part wild, particularly the sea and the sky, the floods of light from the stars, and the warm, unspoilable heart of the earth, infinitely beautiful, though only dimly visible to the eye of imagination. The geysers, too, spouting from the hot underworld; the steady, long-lasting glaciers on the mountains, obedient only to the sun; Yosemite domes and the tremendous grandeur of rocky cañons and mountains in general,—these must always be wild, for man can change them and mar them hardly more than can the butterflies that hover above them. But the continent's outer beauty is fast passing away, especially the plant part of it, the most destructible and most universally charming of all.

Only thirty years ago, the great Central Valley of California, five hundred miles long and fifty miles wide, was one bed of golden and purple flowers. Now it is ploughed and pastured out of existence, gone forever,—scarce a memory of it left in fence corners and along the bluffs of the streams. The gardens of the Sierra also, and the noble forests in both the reserved and the unreserved portions, are sadly hacked and trampled, notwithstanding the ruggedness of the topography,—all excepting those of the parks guarded by a few soldiers. In the noblest forests of the world, the ground, once divinely beautiful, is desolate and repulsive, like a face ravaged by disease. This is true also of many other Pacific Coast and Rocky Mountain valleys and forests. The same fate, sooner or later, is awaiting them all, unless awakening public opinion comes forward to stop it. Even the great deserts in Arizona. Nevada, Utah, and New Mexico, which offer so little to attract settlers, and which a few years ago pioneers were afraid of, as places of desolation and death, are now taken as pastures at the rate of one or two square miles per cow, and of course their plant treasures are passing away,—the delicate abronias, phloxes, gilias, etc. Only a few of the bitter, thorny, unbitable shrubs are left, and the sturdy cactuses that defend themselves with bayonets and spears.

Most of the wild plant wealth of the East also has vanished,—gone into dusty history. Only vestiges of its glorious prairie and woodland wealth remain to bless humanity in boggy, rocky, unploughable places. Fortunately, some of these are purely wild, and go far to keep Nature's love visible. White water-lilies, with rootstocks deep and safe in mud, still send up every summer a Milky Way of starry, fragrant flowers around a thousand lakes, and many a tuft of wild grass waves its panicles on mossy rocks, beyond reach of trampling feet, in company with saxifrages, bluebells, and ferns. Even in the midst of farmers' fields, precious sphagnum bogs, too soft for the feet of cattle, are preserved with their charming plants unchanged,— chiogenes, Andromeda, Kalmia, Linnaea, Arethusa, etc. Calypso borealis still hides in the arbor vitæ swamps of Canada, and away to the southward there are a few unspoiled swamps, big ones, where miasma, snakes, and alligators, like guardian angels, defend their treasures and keep them pure as paradise. And beside a' that and a' that, the East is blessed with good winters and blossoming clouds that shed white flowers over all the land, covering every scar and making the saddest landscape divine at least once a year.

The most extensive, least spoiled, and most unspoilable of the gardens of the continent are the vast tundras of Alaska. In summer they extend smooth, even, undulating, continuous beds of flowers and leaves from about lat. 62° to the shores of the Arctic Ocean; and in winter sheets of snowflowers make all the country shine, one mass of white radiance like a star. Nor are these Arctic plant people the pitiful frost-pinched unfortunates they are guessed to be by those who have never seen them. Though lowly in stature, keeping near the frozen ground as if loving it, they are bright and cheery, and speak Nature's love as plainly as their big relatives of the south. Tenderly happed and tucked in beneath downy snow to sleep through the long white winter, they make haste to bloom in the spring without trying to grow tall, though some rise high enough to ripple and wave in the wind, and display masses of color—yellow, purple, and blue—so rich that they look like beds of rainbows, and are visible miles and miles away. . . .

In the meantime, the wildest health and pleasure grounds accessible and available to tourists seeking escape from care and dust and early death are the parks and reservations of the West. There are four national parks,—the Yellowstone, Yosemite, General Grant, and Sequoia,—all within easy reach, and thirty forest reservations, a magnificent realm of woods, most of which, by railroads and trails and open ridges, is also fairly accessible, not only to the determined traveler rejoicing in difficulties, but to those (may their tribe increase) who, not tired, not sick, just naturally take wing every summer in search of wildness. The forty million acres of these reserves are in the main unspoiled as yet, though sadly wasted and threatened on their more open margins by the axe and fire of the lumberman and prospector, and by hoofed locusts, which, like the winged ones, devour every leaf within reach, while the shepherds and owners set fires with the intention of making a blade of grass grow in the place of every tree, but with the result of killing both the grass and the trees. . . .

The Rocky Mountain reserves are the Teton, Yellowstone, Lewis and Clark, Bitter Root, Priest River, and Flathead, comprehending more than twelve million acres of mostly unclaimed, rough, forest-covered mountains in which the great rivers of the country take their rise. The commonest tree in most of them is the brave, indomitable, and altogether admirable Pinus contorta, widely distributed in all kinds of climate and soil, growing cheerily in frosty Alaska, breathing the damp salt air of the sea as well as the dry biting blasts of the Arctic interior, and making itself at home on the most dangerous flame-swept slopes and ridges of the Rocky Mountains in immeasurable abundance and variety of forms. Thousands of acres of this species are destroyed by running fires nearly every summer, but a new growth springs quickly from the ashes. It is generally small, and yields few sawlogs of commercial value, but is of incalculable importance to the farmer and miner; supplying fencing, mine timbers, and firewood, holding the porous soil on steep slopes, preventing landslips and avalanches, and giving kindly nourishing shelter to animals and the widely outspread sources of the life-giving rivers. The other trees are mostly spruce, mountain pine, cedar, juniper, larch, and balsam fir; some of them, especially on the western slopes of the mountains, attaining grand size and furnishing abundance of fine timber.

Perhaps the least known of all this grand group of reserves is the Bitter Root, of more than four million acres. It is the wildest, shaggiest block of forest wildness in the Rocky Mountains, full of happy, healthy, storm-loving trees, full of streams that dance and sing in glorious array, and full of Nature's animals,—elk, deer, wild sheep, bears, cats, and innumerable smaller people. . . .

The vast Pacific Coast reserves in Washington and Oregon—the Cascade, Washington, Mount Rainier, Olympic, Bull Run, and Ashland, named in order of size—include more than

12,500,000 acres of magnificent forests of beautiful and gigantic trees. They extend over the wild, unexplored Olympic Mountains and both flanks of the Cascade Range, the wet and the dry. On the east side of the Cascades the woods are sunny and open, and contain principally yellow pine, of moderate size, but of great value as a cover for the irrigating streams that flow into the dry interior, where agriculture on a grand scale is being carried on. Along the moist, balmy, foggy, west flank of the mountains, facing the sea, the woods reach their highest development, and, excepting the California redwoods, are the heaviest on the continent. They are made up mostly of the Douglas spruce (Pseudotsuga taxifolia), with the giant arbor vitæ, or cedar, and several species of fir and hemlock in varying abundance, forming a forest kingdom unlike any other, in which limb meets limb, touching and overlapping in bright, lively, triumphant exuberance, 250, 300, and even 400 feet above the shady, mossy ground. Over all the other species the Douglas spruce reigns supreme. It is not only a large tree, the tallest in America next to the redwood, but a very beautiful one, with bright green drooping foliage, handsome pendent cones, and a shaft exquisitely straight and round and regular. Forming extensive forests by itself in many places, it lifts its spiry tops into the sky close together with as even a growth as a well-tilled field of grain. And no ground has been better tilled for wheat than these Cascade Mountains for trees: they were ploughed by mighty glaciers, and harrowed and mellowed and outspread by the broad streams that flowed from the ice-ploughs as they were withdrawn at the close of the glacial period.

In proportion to its weight when dry, Douglas spruce timber is perhaps stronger than that of any other large conifer in the country, and being tough, durable, and elastic, it is admirably suited for ship-building, piles, and heavy timbers in general; but its hardness and liability to warp when it is cut into boards render it unfit for fine work. In the lumber markets of California it is called "Oregon pine." When lumbering is going on in the best Douglas woods, especially about Puget Sound, many of the long slender boles are saved for spars; and so superior is their quality that they are called for in almost every shipyard in the world, and it is interesting to follow their fortunes. Felled and peeled and dragged to tide-water, they are raised again as yards and masts for ships, given iron roots and canvas foliage, decorated with flags, and sent to sea, where in glad motion they go cheerily over the ocean prairie in every latitude and longitude, singing and bowing responsive to the same winds that waved them when they were in the woods. After standing in one place for centuries they thus go round the world like tourists, meeting many a friend from the old home forest; some traveling like themselves, some standing head downward in muddy harbors, holding up the platforms of wharves, and others doing all kinds of hard timber work, showy or hidden.

This wonderful tree also grows far northward in British Columbia, and southward along the coast and middle regions of Oregon and California; flourishing with the redwood wherever it can find an opening, and with the sugar pine, yellow pine, and libocedrus in the Sierra. It extends into the San Gabriel, San Bernardino, and San Jacinto Mountains of southern California. It also grows well in the Wasatch Mountains, where it is called "red pine," and on many parts of the Rocky Mountains and short interior ranges of the Great Basin. But though thus widely distributed, only in Oregon, Washington, and some parts of British Columbia does it reach perfect development. . . .

The Mount Rainier forest reserve should be made a national park and guarded while yet its bloom is on; for if in the making of the West Nature had what we call parks in mind,— places for rest, inspiration, and prayers,—this Rainier region must surely be one of them. In the centre of it there is a lonely mountain capped with ice; from the ice-cap glaciers radiate in every direction, and young rivers from the glaciers; while its flanks, sweeping down in beautiful curves, are clad with forests and gardens, and filled with birds and animals. Specimens of the best of Nature's treasures have been lovingly gathered here and arranged in simple symmetrical beauty within regular bounds.

Of all the fire-mountains which like beacons once blazed along the Pacific Coast, Mount Rainier is the noblest in form, has the most interesting forest cover, and, with perhaps the exception of Shasta, is the highest and most flowery. Its massive white dome rises out of its forests, like a world by itself, to a height of fourteen thousand to fifteen thousand feet. The forests reach to a height of a little over six thousand feet, and above the forests there is a zone of the loveliest flowers, fifty miles in circuit and nearly two miles wide, so closely planted and luxuriant that it seems as if Nature, glad to make an open space between woods so dense and ice so deep, were economizing the precious ground, and trying to see how many of her darlings she can get together in one mountain wreath,— daisies, anemones, geraniums, columbines, erythroniums, larkspurs, etc., among which we wade knee-deep and waist-deep, the bright corollas in myriads touching petal to petal. Picturesque detached groups of the spiry Abies subalpina stand like islands along the lower margin of the garden zone, while on the upper margin there are extensive beds of bryanthus, Cassiope, Kalmia, and other heathworts, and higher still saxifrages and drabas, more and more lowly, reach up to the edge of the ice. Altogether this is the richest subalpine garden I ever found, a perfect floral elysium. The icy dome needs none of man's care, but unless the reserve is guarded the flower bloom will soon be killed, and nothing of the forests will be left but black stump monuments.

The Sierra of California is the most openly beautiful and useful of all the forest reserves, and the largest, excepting the Cascade Reserve of Oregon and the Bitter Root of Montana and Idaho. It embraces over four million acres of the grandest scenery and grandest trees on the continent, and its forests are planted just where they do the most good, not only for beauty, but for farming in the great San Joaquin Valley beneath them. It extends southward from the Yosemite National Park to the end of the range, a distance of nearly two hundred miles. No other coniferous forest in the world contains so many species or so many large and beautiful trees,—Sequoia gigantea, king of conifers, "the noblest of a noble race," as Sir Joseph Hooker well says; the sugar pine, king of all the world's pines, living or extinct; the yellow pine, next in rank, which here reaches most perfect development, forming noble towers of verdure two hundred feet high; the mountain pine, which braves the coldest blasts far up the mountains on grim, rocky slopes; and five others, flourishing each in its place, making eight species of pine in one forest, which is still further enriched by the great Douglas spruce, libocedrus, two species of silver fir, large trees and exquisitely beautiful, the Paton hemlock, the most graceful of evergreens, the curious tumion, oaks of many species, maples, alders, poplars, and flowering dogwood, all fringed with flowery underbrush, manzanita, ceanothus, wild rose, cherry, chestnut, and rhododendron. Wandering at random through these friendly, approachable woods, one comes here and there to the loveliest lily gardens, some of the lilies ten feet high, and the smoothest gentian meadows, and Yosemite valley known only to mountaineers. Once I spent a night by a camp-fire on Mount Shasta with Asa Gray and Sir Joseph Hooker, and, knowing that they were acquainted with all the great forests of the world, I asked whether they knew any coniferous forest that rivaled that of the Sierra. They unhesitatingly said "No. In the beauty and grandeur of individual trees, and in number and variety of species, the Sierra forests surpass all others."

This Sierra Reserve, proclaimed by the President of the United States in September, 1893, is worth the most thoughtful care of the government for its own sake, without considering its value as the fountain of the rivers on which the fertility of the great San Joaquin Valley depends. Yet it gets no care at all. In the fog of tariff, silver, and annexation politics it is left wholly unguarded, though the management of the adjacent national parks by a few soldiers shows how well and how easily it can be preserved. In the meantime, lumbermen are allowed to spoil it at their will, and sheep in uncountable ravenous hordes to trample it and devour every green leaf within reach; while the shepherds, like destroying angels, set innumerable fires, which burn not only the undergrowth of seedlings on which the permanence of the forest depends, but countless thousands of the venerable giants. If every citizen could take one walk through this reserve, there would be no more trouble about its care; for only in darkness does vandalism flourish.

The reserves of southern California,—the San Gabriel, San Bernardino, San Jacinto, and Trabuco,—though not large, only about two million acres altogether, are perhaps the best appreciated. Their slopes are covered with a close, almost impenetrable growth of flowery bushes, beginning on the sides of the fertile coast valleys and the dry interior plains. Their higher ridges, however, and mountains are open, and fairly well forested with sugar pine, yellow pine, Douglas spruce, libocedrus, and white fir. As timber fountains they amount to little, but as bird and bee pastures, cover for the precious streams that irrigate the lowlands, and quickly available retreats from dust and heat and care, their value is incalculable. Good roads have been graded into them, by which in a few hours lowlanders can get well up into the sky and find refuge in hospitable camps and club-houses, where, while breathing reviving ozone, they may absorb the beauty about them, and look comfortably down on the busy towns and the most beautiful orange groves ever planted since gardening began.

The Grand Cañon Reserve of Arizona, of nearly two million acres, or the most interesting part of it, as well as the Rainier region, should be made into a national park, on account of their supreme grandeur and beauty. Setting out from Flagstaff, a station on the Atchison, Topeka, and Santa Fé Railroad, on the way to the cañon you pass through beautiful forests of yellow pine,—like those of the Black Hills, but more extensive,—and curious dwarf forests of nut pine and juniper, the spaces between the miniature trees planted with many interesting species of eriogonum, yucca, and cactus. After riding or walking seventy-five miles through these pleasure-grounds, the San Francisco and other mountains, abounding in flowery parklike openings and smooth shallow valleys with long vistas which in fineness of finish and arrangement suggest the work of a consummate landscape artist, watching you all the way, you come to the most tremendous cañon in the world. It is abruptly countersunk in the forest plateau, so that you see nothing of it until you are suddenly stopped on its brink, with its immeasurable wealth of divinely colored and sculptured buildings before you and beneath you. No matter how far you have wandered hitherto, or how many famous gorges and valleys you have seen, this one, the Grand Cañon of the Colorado, will seem as novel to you, as unearthly in the color and grandeur and quantity of its architecture, as if you had found it after death, on some other star; so incomparably lovely and grand and supreme is it above all the other cañons in our fire-moulded, earthquake-shaken, rain-washed, wave-washed, river and glacier sculptured world. It is about six thousand feet deep where you first see it, and from rim to rim ten to fifteen miles wide. Instead of being dependent for interest upon waterfalls, depth, wall sculpture, and beauty of parklike floor, like most other great cañons, it has no waterfalls in sight, and no appreciable floor spaces. The big river has just room enough to flow and roar obscurely, here and there groping its way as best it can, like a weary, murmuring, overladen traveler trying to escape from the tremendous, bewildering labyrinthic abyss, while its roar serves only to deepen the silence. Instead of being filled with air, the vast space between the walls is crowded with Nature's grandest buildings,—a sublime city of them, painted in every color, and adorned with richly fretted cornice and battlement spire and tower in endless variety of style and architecture. Every architectural invention of man has been anticipated, and far more, in this grandest of God's terrestrial cities.

Ethics Must Inform Environmental Thinking

ALDO LEOPOLD

Aldo Leopold is often considered a link between the early conservation movement and post World War II environmentalism. He began his career with the U.S. Forest Service and expanded on Gifford Pinchot's doctrine of the "wise use" of nature by arguing for
a "land ethic." Ethics engage a sense of responsibility to others in a
community, he argued, and humans need to include nature as part
of that community. In the decades since their publication in 1949,
his ideas have become increasingly representative of environmental views today.

When god-like Odysseus returned from the wars in
Troy, he hanged all on one rope a dozen slave-girls of
his household whom he suspected of misbehavior during his
absence.

This hanging involved no question of propriety. The girls
were property. The disposal of property was then, as now, a
matter of expediency, not of right and wrong.

Concepts of right and wrong were not lacking from
Odysseus' Greece: witness the fidelity of his wife through the
long years before at last his black-prowed galleys clove the
wine-dark seas for home. The ethical structure of that day covered wives, but had not yet been extended to human chattels.
During the three thousand years which have since elapsed, ethical criteria have been extended to many fields of conduct, with
corresponding shrinkages in those judged by expediency only.

THE ETHICAL SEQUENCE

This extension of ethics, so far studied only by philosophers, is actually a process in ecological evolution. Its sequences may be described in ecological as well as in philosophical terms. An ethic, ecologically, is a limitation on freedom of action in the struggle for existence. An ethic, philosophically, is a differentiation of social from anti-social conduct. These are two definitions of one thing. The thing has its origin in the tendency of interdependent individuals or groups to evolve modes of co-operation. The ecologist calls these symbioses. Politics and economics are advanced symbioses in which the original free-for-all competition has been replaced, in part, by co-operative mechanisms with an ethical content.

The complexity of co-operative mechanisms has increased with population density, and with the efficiency of tools. It was simpler, for example, to define the anti-social uses of sticks and stones in the days of the mastodons than of bullets and billboards in the age of motors.

The first ethics dealt with the relation between individuals; the Mosaic Decalogue is an example. Later accretions dealt with the relation between the individual and society. The Golden Rule tries to integrate the individual to society; democracy to integrate social organization to the individual.

There is as yet no ethic dealing with man's relation to land and to the animals and plants which grow upon it. Land, like Odysseus' slave-girls, is still property. The land-relation is still strictly economic, entailing privileges but not obligations.

The extension of ethics to this third element in human environment is, if I read the evidence correctly, an evolutionary possibility and an ecological necessity. It is the third step in a sequence. The first two have already been taken. Individual thinkers since the days of Ezekiel and Isaiah have asserted that the despoliation of land is not only inexpedient but wrong. Society, however, has not yet affirmed their belief. I regard the present conservation movement as the embryo of such an affirmation.

An ethic may be regarded as a mode of guidance for meeting ecological situations so new or intricate, or involving such deferred reactions, that the path of social expediency is not discernible to the average individual. Animal instincts are modes of guidance for the individual in meeting such situations. Ethics are possibly a kind of community instinct in-the-making.

The Community Concept

All ethics so far evolved rest upon a single premise: that the individual is a member of a community of interdependent parts. His instincts prompt him to compete for his place in that community, but his ethics prompt him also to co-operate (perhaps in order that there may be a place to compete for).

The land ethic simply enlarges the boundaries of the community to include soils, waters, plants, and animals, or collectively: the land.

This sounds simple: do we not already sing our love for and obligation to the land of the free and the home of the brave? Yes, but just what and whom do we love? Certainly not the soil, which we are sending helter-skelter downriver. Certainly not the waters, which we assume have no function except to turn turbines, float barges, and carry off sewage. Certainly not the plants, of which we exterminate whole communities without batting an eye. Certainly not the animals, of which we have already extirpated many of the largest and most beautiful species. A land ethic of course cannot prevent the alteration, management, and use of these 'resources' but it does affirm their right to continued existence, and, at least in spots, their continued existence in a natural state.

In short, a land ethic changes the role of *Homo sapiens* from conqueror of the land-community to plain member and citizen of it. It implies respect for his fellow-members, and also respect for the community as such.

In human history, we have learned (I hope) that the conqueror role is eventually self-defeating. Why? Because it is implicit in such a role that the conqueror knows, *ex cathedra,* just what makes the community clock tick, and just what and who is valuable, and what and who is worthless, in community life.

It always turns out that he knows neither, and this is why his conquests eventually defeat themselves.

In the biotic community, a parallel situation exists. Abraham knew exactly what the land was for: it was to drip milk and honey into Abraham's mouth. At the present moment, the assurance with which we regard this assumption is inverse to the degree of our education.

The ordinary citizen today assumes that science knows what makes the community clock tick; the scientist is equally sure that he does not. He knows that the biotic mechanism is so complex that its workings may never be fully understood.

That man is, in fact, only a member of a biotic team is shown by an ecological interpretation of history. Many historical events, hitherto explained solely in terms of human enterprise, were actually biotic interactions between people and land. The characteristics of the land determined the facts quite as potently as the characteristics of the men who lived on it.

Consider, for example, the settlement of the Mississippi valley. In the years following the Revolution, three groups were contending for its control: the native Indian, the French and English traders, and the American settlers. Historians wonder what would have happened if the English at Detroit had thrown a little more weight into the Indian side of those tipsy scales which decided the outcome of the colonial migration into the cane-lands of Kentucky. It is time now to ponder the fact that the cane-lands, when subjected to the particular mixture of forces represented by the cow, plow, fire, and axe of the pioneer, became bluegrass. What if the plant succession inherent in this dark and bloody ground had, under the impact of these forces, given us some worthless sedge, shrub, or weed? Would Boone and Kenton have held out? Would there have been any overflow into Ohio, Indiana, Illinois, and Missouri? Any Louisiana Purchase? Any transcontinental union of new states? Any Civil War?

Kentucky was one sentence in the drama of history. We are commonly told what the human actors in this drama tried to do, but we are seldom told that their success, or the lack of it, hung in large degree on the reaction of particular soils to the impact of the particular forces exerted by their occupancy. In the case of Kentucky, we do not even know where the blue-grass came from—whether it is a native species, or a stowaway from Europe.

Contrast the cane-lands with what hindsight tells us about the Southwest, where the pioneers were equally brave, re-sourceful, and persevering. The impact of occupancy here brought no bluegrass, or other plant fitted to withstand the bumps and buffetings of hard use. This region, when grazed by livestock, reverted through a series of more and more worthless grasses, shrubs, and weeds to a condition of unstable equilibrium. Each recession of plant types bred erosion; each increment to erosion bred a further recession of plants. The result today is a progressive and mutual deterioration, not only of plants and soils, but of the animal community subsisting thereon. The early settlers did not expect this: on the ciénegas of New Mexico some even cut ditches to hasten it. So subtle has been its progress that few residents of the region are aware of it. It is quite invisible to the tourist who finds this wrecked landscape colorful and charming (as indeed it is, but it bears scant resemblance to what it was in 1848).

This same landscape was 'developed' once before, but with quite different results. The Pueblo Indians settled the South-west in pre-Colombian times, but they happened *not* to be equipped with range livestock. Their civilization expired, but not because their land expired.

In India, regions devoid of any sod-forming grass have been settled, apparently without wrecking the land, by the simple expedient of carrying the grass to the cow, rather than vice versa. (Was this the result of some deep wisdom, or was it just good luck? I do not know.)

In short, the plant succession steered the course of history; the pioneer simply demonstrated, for good or ill, what succes-sions inhered in the land. Is history taught in this spirit? It will be, once the concept of land as a community really penetrates our intellectual life.

Wilderness Should Be Preserved for Its Own Sake

WALLACE STEGNER

Writing for a research center created by Congress, Wallace Stegner projected in the early 1960s the recreational needs of the American public between 1976 and 2000. In this "wilderness letter" he argues that wilderness is valuable not just as a genetic reserve, or for recreation, but that it is valuable for its own sake. Humans are a wild species, never bred by another species, never domesticated by outsiders. When they lose the wilderness they lose something of their selves. While his arguments are highly literary and somewhat vague, it is precisely these hard-to-define sentiments that persuaded the American public to take action. Only a few years after he wrote this piece, Congress passed a law establishing the National Wilderness Preservation System, in 1964.

I should like to urge some arguments for wilderness preservation that involve recreation, as it is ordinarily conceived, hardly at all. Hunting, fishing, hiking, mountain-climbing, camping, photography, and the enjoyment of natural scenery will all, surely, figure in your report. So will the wilderness as a genetic reserve, a scientific yardstick by which we may measure the world in its natural balance against the world in its man-made imbalance. What I want to speak for is not so much the wilderness uses, valuable as those are, but the wilderness *idea,* which is a resource in itself. Being an intangible and spiritual resource, it will seem mystical to the practical-minded—

From Wallace Stegner's "Wilderness Letter," to David Pesonen of the Outdoor Recreation Resources Review Commission, December 3, 1960, available at www.wilderness.org/ standbylands/wilderness/wildletter2.htm. Reprinted with permission.

but then anything that cannot be moved by a bulldozer is likely to seem mystical to them.

SPEAKING FOR THE WILDERNESS IDEA

I want to speak for the wilderness idea as something that has helped form our character and that has certainly shaped our history as a people. It has no more to do with recreation than churches have to do with recreation, or than the strenuousness and optimism and expansiveness of what historians call the "American Dream" have to do with recreation. Nevertheless, since it is only in this recreation survey that the values of wilderness are being compiled, I hope you will permit me to insert this idea between the leaves, as it were, of the recreation report.

Something will have gone out of us as a people if we ever let the remaining wilderness be destroyed; if we permit the last virgin forests to be turned into comic books and plastic cigarette cases; if we drive the few remaining members of the wild species into zoos or to extinction; if we pollute the last clear air and dirty the last clean streams and push our paved roads through the last of the silence, so that never again will Americans be free in their own country from the noise, the exhausts, the stinks of human and automotive waste. And so that never again can we have the chance to see ourselves single, separate, vertical and individual in the world, part of the environment of trees and rocks and soil, brother to the other animals, part of the natural world and competent to belong in it. Without any remaining wilderness we are committed wholly, without chance for even momentary reflection and rest, to a headlong drive into our technological termite-life, the Brave New World of a completely man-controlled environment. We need wilderness preserved—as much of it as is still left, and as many kinds—because it was the challenge against which our character as a people was formed. The reminder and the reassurance that it is still there is good for our spiritual health even if we never once in ten years set foot in it. It is good for us when we are young, because of the incomparable sanity it can bring briefly, as vacation and rest, into our insane lives. It is important to us when we are old simply because it is there—important, that is, simply as idea.

We are a wild species, as Darwin pointed out. Nobody ever tamed or domesticated or scientifically bred us. But for at least three millennia we have been engaged in a cumulative and ambitious race to modify and gain control of our environment, and in the process we have come close to domesticating ourselves. Not many people are likely, any more, to look upon what we call "progress" as an unmixed blessing. Just as surely as it has brought us increased comfort and more material goods, it has brought us spiritual losses, and it threatens now to become the Frankenstein that will destroy us. One means of sanity is to retain a hold on the natural world, to remain, insofar as we can, good animals. Americans still have that chance, more than many peoples; for while we were demonstrating ourselves the most efficient and ruthless environment-busters in history, and slashing and burning and cutting our way through a wilderness continent, the wilderness was working on us. It remains in us as surely as Indian names remain on the land. If the abstract dream of human liberty and human dignity became, in America, something more than an abstract dream, mark it down at least partially to the fact that we were in subtle ways subdued by what we conquered.

The Connecticut Yankee, sending likely candidates from King Arthur's unjust kingdom to his Man Factory for rehabilitation, was overoptimistic, as he later admitted. These things cannot be forced, they have to grow. To make such a man, such a democrat, such a believer in human individual dignity, as Mark Twain himself, the frontier was necessary, Hannibal and the Mississippi and Virginia City, and reaching out from those the wilderness: the wilderness as opportunity and as idea, the thing that has helped to make an American different from and, until we forget it in the roar of our industrial cities, more fortunate than other men. For an American, insofar as he is new and different at all, is a civilized man who has renewed himself in the wild. The American experience has been the confrontation of old peoples and cultures by a world as new as if it had just arisen from the sea. That gave us our hope and our excitement, and the hope and excitement can be passed on to newer Americans; Americans who never saw any phase of the frontier. But only so long as we keep the remainder of our wild as a reserve and a promise—a sort of wilderness bank.

As a novelist, I may perhaps be forgiven for taking literature as a reflection, indirect but profoundly true, of our national consciousness. And our literature, as perhaps you are aware, is sick, embittered, losing its mind, losing its faith. Our novelists are the declared enemies of their society. There has hardly been a serious or important novel in this century that did not repudiate in part or in whole American technological culture for its commercialism, its vulgarity, and the way in which it has dirtied a clean continent and a clean dream. I do not expect that the preservation of our remaining wilderness is going to cure this condition. But the mere example that we can as a nation apply some other criteria than commercial and exploitative considerations would be heartening to many Americans, novelists or otherwise. We need to demonstrate our acceptance of the natural world, including ourselves; we need the spiritual refreshment that being natural can produce. And one of the best places for us to get that is in the wilderness where the fun houses, the bulldozers, and the pavements of our civilization are shut out.

Sherwood Anderson, in a letter to Waldo Frank in the 1920s, said it better than I can. 'Is it not likely that when the country was new and men were often alone in the fields and the forest they got a sense of bigness outside themselves that has now in some way been lost? ... Mystery whispered in the grass, played in the branches of trees overhead, was caught up and blown across the American line in clouds of dust at evening on the prairies ... I am old enough to remember tales that strengthen my belief in a deep semi-religious influence that was formerly at work among our people. The flavor of it hangs over the best work of Mark Twain ... I can remember old fellows in my home town speaking feelingly of an evening spent on the big empty plains. It had taken the shrillness out of them. They had learned the trick of quiet. . . .

We could learn it too, even yet; even our children and grandchildren could learn it. But only if we save, for just such absolutely nonrecreational, impractical, and mystical uses as this, all the wild that still remains to us.

TURNING FROM HOPE TO BITTERNESS

It seems to me significant that the distinct downturn in our literature from hope to bitterness took place almost at the precise time when the frontier officially came to an end, in 1890, and when the American way of life had begun to turn strongly urban and industrial. The more urban it has become, and the more frantic with technological change, the sicker and more embittered our literature, and I believe our people, have become. For myself, I grew up on the empty plains of Saskatchewan and Montana and in the mountains of Utah, and I put a very high valuation on what those places gave me. And if I had not been able periodically to renew myself in the mountains and deserts of Western America I would be very nearly bughouse. Even when I can't get to the back country, the thought of the colored deserts of southern Utah, or the reassurance that there are still stretches of prairie where the world can be instantaneously perceived as disk and bowl, and where the little but intensely important human being is exposed to the five directions and the thirty-six winds, is a positive consolation. The idea alone can sustain me. But as the wilderness areas are progressively exploited or 'improved,' as the jeeps and bulldozers of uranium prospectors scar up the deserts and the roads are cut into the alpine timberlands, and as the remnants of the unspoiled and natural world are progressively eroded, every such loss is a little death in me. In us.

Nevertheless I am not moved by the argument that those wilderness areas which have already been exposed to grazing or mining are already deflowered, and so might as well be 'harvested.' For mining I cannot say much good except that its operations are generally short-lived. The extractable wealth is taken and the shafts, the tailings, and the ruins left, and in a dry country such as the American West the wounds men make in the earth do not quickly heal. Still, they are only wounds; they aren't absolutely mortal. Better a wounded wilderness than none at all. And as for grazing, if it is strictly controlled so that it does not destroy the ground cover, damage the ecology, or compete with the wildlife it is in itself nothing that need conflict with the wilderness feeling or the validity of the wilderness experience. I have known enough range cattle to recognize them as wild animals; and the people who herd them have, in the wilderness context, the dignity of rareness; they belong on the frontier, moreover, and have a look of rightness. The invasion they make on the virgin country is a sort of invasion that is as old as Neanderthal man, and they can, in moderation, even emphasize a man's feeling of belonging to the natural world. Under surveillance, they can belong; under control, they need not deface or mar. I do not believe that in wilderness areas where grazing has never been permitted, it should be permitted; but I do not believe either that an otherwise untouched wilderness should be eliminated from the preservation plan because of limited existing uses such as grazing which are in consonance with the frontier condition and image....

A LOVELY AND TERRIBLE WILDERNESS

So are great reaches of our western deserts, scarred somewhat by prospectors but otherwise open, beautiful, waiting, close to whatever God you want to see in them. Just as a sample, let me suggest the Robbers' Roost country in Wayne County, Utah, near the Capitol Reef National Monument. In that desert climate the dozer and jeep tracks will not soon melt back into the earth, but the country has a way of making the scars insignificant. It is a lovely and terrible wilderness, such a wilderness as Christ and the prophets went out into; harshly and beautifully colored, broken and worn until its bones are exposed, its great sky without a smudge or taint from Technocracy, and in hidden corners and pockets under its cliffs the sudden poetry of springs. Save a piece of country like that intact, and it does not matter in the slightest that only a few people every year will go into it. That is precisely its value. Roads would be a desecration, crowds would ruin it. But those who haven't the strength or youth to go into it and live with it can still drive up onto the shoulder of the Aquarius Plateau and simply sit and look. They can look two hundred miles, clear into Colorado; and looking down over the cliffs and canyons of the San Rafael Swell and the Robbers' Roost they can also look as deeply into themselves as anywhere I know. And if they can't even get to the places on the Aquarius where the present roads will carry them, they can simply contemplate the *idea,* take pleasure in the fact that such a timeless and un-controlled part of earth is still there.

These are some of the things wilderness can do for us. That is the reason we need to put into effect, for its preservation, some other principle than the principles of exploitation or usefulness or even recreation. We simply need that wild country available to us, even if we never do more than drive to its edge and look in. For it can be a means of reassuring ourselves of our sanity as creatures, a part of the geography of hope.

CHAPTER 4

THE GREEN MOVEMENT

AMERICAN
SOCIAL
MOVEMENTS

Evergreen

GARY SNYDER

Poet Gary Snyder was born in San Francisco and raised in the forests of the Northwest. During the 1950s Snyder took on a variety of odd jobs to support himself writing poetry. In this viewpoint, Snyder speaks for many in the environmental movement when he notes the need to reconnect humans to a sense of place and community with nature. Snyder's work emphasizes an awareness of the local ecological community and spiritually attempts to return people to a sense of the sacredness of life through reverent interaction with our environment. He pioneers a genre that mixes descriptive writing with scientific analysis and clear, specific environmental advocacy.

The raw dry country of the American West had an odd effect on American politics. It transformed and even radicalized some people. Once the West was closed to homesteading and the unclaimed lands became public domain, a few individuals realized that the future of these lands was open to public discussion. Some went from exploration and appreciation of wilderness to political activism.

INSTRUCTION FROM THE USELESS

Daoist philosophers tell us that surprise and subtle instruction might come forth from the Useless. So it was with the wastelands of the American West—inaccessible, inhospitable, arid, and forbidding to the eyes of most early Euro-Americans. The Useless Lands became the dreaming place of a few nineteenth- and early-twentieth-century men and women (John Wesley Powell on matters of water and public lands, Mary Austin on Native Americans, deserts, women) who went out into the space and loneliness and returned from their quests not only to criticize the policies and assumptions of the expanding United States but, in the name of wilderness and the commons, to hoist the sails that are filling with wind today. Some of the newly established public lands did have potential uses for lumber, grazing, and mining. But in the case of timber and grass, the best lands were already in private hands. What went into the public domain (or occasionally into Indian reservation status) was—by the standards of those days—marginal land. The off-limits bombing ranges and nuclear test sites of the Great Basin are public domain lands, too, borrowed by the military from the BLM [Bureau of Land Management].

So the forests that were set aside for the initial Forest Reserves were not at that time considered prime timber land. Early-day lumber interests in the Pacific Northwest went for the dense, low-elevation conifer forests like those around the house I grew up in or those forests right on saltwater or near rivers. This accessible land, once clearcut, became real estate, but the farther reaches were kept by the big companies as commercial forest. Much of the Olympic Peninsula forest land is privately held. Only by luck and chance did an occasional low-elevation stand such as the Hoh River forest in Olympic National Park, or Jedediah Smith redwoods in California, end up in public domain. It is by virtue of these islands of forest survivors that we can still see what the primeval forest of the West Coast—in its densest and most concentrated incarnation—was like. "Virgin forest" it was once called, a telling term. Then it was called "old growth" or in certain cases "climax." Now we begin to call it "ancient forest."

On the rainy Pacific slope there were million-acre stands that had been coevolving for millennia, possibly for over a million years. Such forests are the fullest examples of ecological process, containing as they do huge quantities of dead and decaying matter as well as the new green and preserving the energy pathways of both detritus and growth. An ancient forest will have many truly large old trees—some having craggy, broken-topped, mossy "dirty" crowns with much organic accumulation, most with holes and rot in them. There will be standing snags and tons of dead down logs. These characteristics, although not delightful to lumbermen ("overripe"), are what make an ancient forest more than a stand of timber: it is a palace of organisms, a heaven for many beings, a temple where life deeply investigates the puzzle of itself. Living activity goes right down to and under the "ground"—the litter, the duff. There are termites, larvae, millipedes, mites, earthworms, springtails, pillbugs, and the fine threads of fungus woven through. "There are as many as 5,500 individuals (not counting the earthworms and nematodes) per square foot of soil to a depth of 13 inches. As many as 70 different species have been collected from less than a square foot of rich forest soil. The total animal population of the soil and litter together probably approaches 10,000 animals per square foot."

The dominant conifers in this forest, Douglas Fir, Western Red Cedar, Western Hemlock, Noble Fir, Sitka Spruce, and Coastal Redwood, are all long-lived and grow to great size. They are often the longest-lived of their genera. The old forests of the western slopes support some of the highest per-acre biomass—total living matter—the world has seen, approached only by some of the Australian eucalyptus forests. An old-growth temperate hardwood forest, and also the tropical forests, average around 153 tons per acre. The west slope forests of the Oregon Cascades averaged 433 tons per acre. At the very top of the scale, the coastal redwood forests have been as high as 1,831 tons per acre.

Forest ecologists and paleoecologists speculate on how such a massive forest came into existence. It seems the western forest of twenty or so million years ago was largely deciduous hardwoods—ash, maple, beech, oak, chestnut, elm, gingko—with conifers only at the highest elevations. Twelve to eighteen million years ago, the conifers began to occupy larger areas and then made continuous connection with each other along the uplands. By a million and a half years ago, in the early Pleistocene, the conifers had completely taken over and the forest was essentially as it is now. Forests of the type that had prevailed earlier, the hardwoods, survive today in the eastern

United States and were also the original vegetation (before agriculture and early logging) of China and Japan. Visiting Great Smoky Mountains National Park today might give you an idea of what the mountain forests outside the old Chinese capital of Xian, known earlier as Ch'ang-an, looked like in the ninth century.

SUCCESS OF CONIFERS

In the other temperate-zone forests of the world, conifers are a secondary and occasional presence. The success of the West Coast conifers can be attributed, it seems, to a combination of conditions: relatively cool and quite dry summers (which do not serve deciduous trees so well) combined with mild wet winters (during which the conifers continue to photosynthesize) and an almost total absence of typhoons. The enormous size of the trunks helps to store moisture and nutrients against drought years. The forests are steady-growing and productive (from a timber standpoint) while young, and these particular species keep growing and accumulating biomass long after most other temperate-zone trees have reached equilibrium.

Here we find the northern Flying Squirrel (which lives on truffles) and its sacred enemy the Spotted Owl. The Douglas Squirrel (or Chickaree) lives here, as does its sacred enemy the treetop-dashing Pine Marten that can run a squirrel down. Black Bear seeks the grubs in long-dead logs in her steady ambling search. These and hosts of others occupy the deep shady stable halls—less wind, less swing of temperature, steady moisture—of the huge tree groves. There are treetop-dwelling Red-backed Voles who have been two hundred feet high in the canopy for hundreds of generations, some of whom have never descended to the ground. In a way the web that holds it all together is the mycelia, the fungus-threads that mediate between root-tips of plants and chemistry of soils, bringing nutrients in. This association is as old as plants with roots. The whole of the forest is supported by this buried network.

The forests of the maritime Pacific Northwest are the last remaining forests of any size left in the temperate zone. Plato's

Critias passage (¶ III) says: "In the primitive state of the country [Attica] its mountains were high hills covered with soil . . . and there was abundance of wood in the mountains. Of this last the traces still remain, for although some of the mountains now only afford sustenance to bees, not so very long ago there were still to be seen roofs of timber cut from trees growing there . . . and there were many other high trees. . . . Moreover the land reaped the benefit of the annual rainfall, not as now losing the water which flows off the bare earth into the sea." The cautionary history of the Mediterranean forests is well known. Much of this destruction has taken place in recent centuries, but it was already well under way, especially in the lowlands, during the classical period. In neolithic times the whole basin had perhaps 500 million acres of forest. The higher-elevation forests are all that survive, and even they occupy only 30 percent of the mountain zone—about 45 million acres. Some 100 million acres of land once densely covered with pine, oak, ash, laurel, and myrtle now have only traces of vegetation. There is a more sophisticated vocabulary in the Mediterranean for postforest or nonforest plant communities than we have in California (where everything scrubby is called chaparral). *Maquis* is the term for oak, olive, myrtle, and juniper scrub. An assembly of low waxy drought-resistant shrubs is called *garrigue. Batha* is open bare rock and eroding ground with scattered low shrubs and annuals.

People who live there today do not even know that their gray rocky hills were once rich in groves and wildlife. The intensified destruction was a function of the *type* of agriculture. The small self-sufficient peasant farms and their commons began to be replaced by the huge slave-run *latifundia* estates owned in absentia and planned according to central markets. What wildlife was left in the commons might then be hunted out by the new owners, the forest sold for cash, and field crops extended for what they were worth. "The cities of the Mediterranean littoral became deeply involved in an intensive region-wide trade, with cheap manufactured products, intensified markets and factory-like industrial production. . . . These developments in planned colonization, economic planning, world currencies and media for exchange had drastic consequences for the natural vegetation from Spain through to India."

China's lowland hardwood forests gradually disappeared as agriculture spread and were mostly gone by about thirty-five hundred years ago. (The Chinese philosopher Meng-zi commented on the risks of clearcutting in the fourth century B.C.) The composition of the Japanese forest has been altered by centuries of continuous logging. The Japanese sawmills are now geared down to about eight-inch logs. The original deciduous hardwoods are found only in the most remote mountains. The prized aromatic Hinoki (the Japanese chamaecypress), which is essential to shrine and temple buildings, is now so rare that logs large enough for renovating traditional structures must be imported from the West Coast. Here it is known as Port Orford Cedar, found only in southern Oregon and in the Siskiyou Mountains of northern California. It was used for years to make arrow-shafts. Now Americans cannot afford it. No other softwood on earth commands such prices as the Japanese buyers are willing to pay for this species.

Commercial West Coast logging started around the 1870s. For decades it was all below the four-thousand-foot level. That was the era of the two-man saw, the double-bitted axe-cut undercuts, springboards, the kerosene bottle with a hook wired onto it stuck in the bark. Gypo handloggers felled into the salt-water bays of Puget Sound and rafted their logs to the mills. Then came steam donkey-engine yarders and ox teams, dragging the huge logs down corduroy skidroads or using immense wooden logging wheels that held the butt end aloft as the tail of the log dragged. The ox teams were replaced by narrow-gauge trains, and the steam donkeys by diesel. The lower elevations of the West Coast were effectively totally clearcut.

TECHNOLOGY AND FOREST EXPLOITATION

Chris Maser says: "Every increase in the technology of logging and the utilization of wood fiber has expedited the exploitation of forests; thus from 1935 through 1980 the annual volume of timber cut has increased geometrically by 4.7% per year. . . . By the 1970s, 65% of the timber cut occurred above 4,000 feet in elevation, and because the average tree harvested has become progressively younger and smaller, the increase in annual acreage cut has been five times greater than the increase in volume cut during the last 40 years."

During these years the trains were replaced by trucks, and the high-lead yarders in many cases were replaced by the more mobile crawler-tread tractors we call Cats. From the late forties on, the graceful, musical Royal Chinook two-man falling saws were hung up on the walls of the barns, and the gasoline chainsaw became the faller's tool of choice. By the end of World War II the big logging companies had (with a few notable exceptions) managed to overexploit and mismanage their own timberlands and so they now turned to the federal lands, the people's forests, hoping for a bailout. So much for the virtues of private forest landowners—their history is abysmal—but there are still ill-informed privatization romantics who argue that the public lands should be sold to the highest bidders.

San Francisco 2 × 4s
 were the woods around Seattle:
Someone killed and someone built, a house,
 a forest, wrecked or raised
All America hung on a hook
 & burned by men in their own praise.

Before World War II the U.S. Forest Service played the role of a true conservation agency and spoke against the earlier era of clearcutting. It usually required its contractors to do selective logging to high standards. The allowable cut was much smaller. It went from 3.5 billion board feet in 1950 to 13.5 billion feet in 1970. After 1961 the new Forest Service leadership cosied up to the industry, and the older conservation-oriented personnel were washed out in waves through the sixties and seventies. The USFS now hires mostly road-building engineers. Their silviculturists think of themselves as fiber-growing engineers, and some profess to see no difference between a monoculture plantation of even-age seedlings and a wild forest (or so said Tahoe National Forest silviculturist Phil Aune at a public hearing on the management plan in 1986). The public relations people still cycle the conservation rhetoric of the thirties, as though the Forest Service had never permitted a questionable clearcut or sold old-growth timber at a financial loss.

MANAGING FORESTS

The legislative mandate of the Forest Service leaves no doubt about its responsibility to manage the forest lands *as forests*, which means that lumber is only one of the values to be considered. It is clear that the forests must be managed in a way that makes them permanently sustainable. But Congress, the Department of Agriculture, and business combine to find ways around these restraints. *Renewable* is confused with *sustainable* (just because certain organisms keep renewing themselves does not mean they will do so—especially if abused—forever), and *forever*—the length of time a forest should continue to flourish—is changed to mean "about a hundred and fifty years." Despite the overwhelming evidence of mismanagement that environmental groups have brought against the Forest Service bureaucracy, it arrogantly and stubbornly resists what has become a clear public call for change. So much for the icon of "management" with its uncritical acceptance of the economic speed-trip of modern times (generating faster and faster logging rotations in the woods) as against: slow cycles.

We ask for slower rotations, genuine streamside protection, fewer roads, no cuts on steep slopes, only occasional shelterwood cuts, and only the most prudent application of the appropriate smaller clearcut. We call for a return to selective logging, and to all-age trees, and to serious heart and mind for the protection of endangered species. (The Spotted Owl, the Fisher, and the Pine Marten are only part of the picture.) There should be *absolutely no more logging* in the remaining ancient forests. In addition we need the establishment of habitat corridors to keep the old-growth stands from becoming impoverished biological islands.

Many of the people in the U.S. Forest Service would agree that such practices are essential to genuine sustainability. They are constrained by the tight net of exploitative policies forced on them by Congress and industry. With good practices North America could maintain a lumber industry and protect a halfway decent amount of wild forest for ten thousand years. That is about the same number of years as the age of the continuously settled village culture of the Wei River valley in China, a span of time which is not excessive for humans to consider and plan by. As it is, the United States is suffering a net loss of 900,000 acres of forest per year. Of that loss, an estimated 60,000 acres is ancient forest.

IN THE SHELTER OF ANCIENT TREES

The deep woods turn, turn, and turn again. The ancient forests of the West are still around us. All the houses of San Francisco, Eureka, Corvallis, Portland, Seattle, Longview, are built with those old bodies: the 2 × 4s and siding are from the logging of the 1910s and 1920s. Strip the paint in an old San Francisco apartment and you find prime-quality coastal redwood panels. We live out our daily lives in the shelter of ancient trees. Our great-grandchildren will more likely have to live in the shelter of riverbed-aggregate. Then the forests of the past will be truly entirely gone.

Out in the forest it takes about the same number of years as the tree lived for a fallen tree to totally return to the soil. If societies could learn to live by such a pace there would be no shortages, no extinctions. There would be clear streams, and the salmon would always return to spawn.

A virgin
Forest
Is ancient; many-
Breasted,
Stable; at
Climax.

Global Population Will Reach Crisis Proportions by 2050

J. KENNETH SMAIL

In this viewpoint, J. Kenneth Smail argues that the world has seen explosive population growth over the course of the twentieth century, and that this growth will continue well into the twenty-first century. Smail, who is professor of anthropology at Kenyon College, contends that population growth will have disastrous effects on the global environment and on the quality of life.

The main point of this essay is simply stated. Within the next half-century, it will be essential for the human species to have in place a fully operational, flexibly designed, essentially voluntary, broadly equitable, and internationally co-ordinated set of initiatives focused on dramatically reducing the then-current world population by at least two-thirds to three-fourths. Given that even with the best of intentions it will take considerable time, unusual patience, exceptional administrative talent, and consummate diplomatic skill to develop and implement such an undertaking (probably on the order of 25 to 50 years), it is important that this process of voluntary consensus building—local, national, and global—begin now.

The mathematical inevitability that human numbers will continue their dramatic increase over the next two generations (to perhaps 9 billion or more by the year 2050), the high probability that this numerical increase will exacerbate still further the systemic problems that already plague humanity (economic, political, environmental, social, moral, etc.), and the

Excerpted from "Beyond Population Stabilization: The Case for Dramatically Reducing Global Human Numbers," by J. Kenneth Smail, *Politics and Life Sciences*, September 1997. Reprinted with permission.

growing realization that the Earth's long-term carrying capacity may only be sufficient to sustain a global human population in the 2 to 3 billion range (at an "adequate to comfortable" standard of living) only reinforces this sense of urgency.

There are, however, hopeful signs. In recent years, we have finally begun to come to terms with the fact that the consequences of the twentieth century's rapid and seemingly uncontrolled population growth will soon place us—if it has not done so already—in the midst of the greatest crisis our species has yet encountered.

In order better to appreciate the scope and ramifications of this still partly hidden crisis, I shall briefly call attention to ten essential, incontrovertible, and inescapable realities that must not only be fully understood but soon confronted. . . .

THE EXPONENTIAL NATURE OF POPULATION GROWTH

First, during the [twentieth] century world population will have grown from somewhere around 1.6 billion in 1900 to slightly more than 6 billion by the year 2000, an almost four-fold increase in but 100 years. This is an unprecedented numerical expansion. Throughout human history, world population growth measured over similar 100-year intervals has been virtually nonexistent or, at most, modestly incremental; it has only become markedly exponential within the last few hundred years. To illustrate this on a more easily comprehensible scale, based on the present rate of increase of nearly 90 million per year, human population growth during the 1990s alone will amount to nearly one billion, an astonishing 20% increase in but little more than a single decade. Just by itself, this 10 to 11 year increase is equivalent to the total global population in the year 1800 (barely 200 years ago) and is approximately triple the estimated world population (ca. 300 million) at the height of the Roman Empire. It is a chastening thought that even moderate to conservative demographic projections suggest that this billion-per-decade rate of increase will continue well into the [twenty-first] century, and that the current global total of

6.0 billion (late 1999 estimate) could easily reach 9 to 10 billion by mid-twenty-first century.

Second, even if a fully effective program of zero population growth (ZPG) were to be implemented immediately, by limiting human fertility to what demographers term the *replacement rate* (roughly 2.1 children per female), global population would nevertheless continue its rapid rate of expansion. In fact, demographers estimate that it would take at least two to three generations (50 to 75 years) at ZPG fertility levels just to reach a point of population stability, unfortunately at numbers considerably higher than at present. This powerful *population momentum* results from the fact that an unusually high proportion (nearly one-third) of the current world population is under the age of 15 and has not yet reproduced. Even more broad-based population profiles may be found throughout the developing world, where the under-15 age cohort often exceeds 40% and where birth rates have remained high even as mortality rates have fallen. While there are some recent indications that fertility rates are beginning to decline, the current composite for the less-developed world—excluding China—is still nearly double (ca. 3.8) that needed for ZPG.

Third, in addition to fertility levels, it is essential to understand that population growth is also significantly affected by changes in mortality rates. In fact, demographic transition theory suggests that the earlier stages of rapid population expansion are typically fueled more by significant reductions in death rates (i.e., decreased childhood mortality and/or enhanced adult longevity) than by changes in birth rates. Nor does recent empirical data suggest that average human life expectancy has reached anywhere near its theoretical upper limit, in either the developing or developed worlds. Consequently, unless there appears a deadly pandemic, a devastating world war or a massive breakdown in public health (or a combination of all three), it is obvious that ongoing global gains in human longevity will continue to make a major contribution to world population expansion over the next half-century, regardless of whatever progress might be made in reducing fertility.

A further consequence of this continuing trend is the fact that most national populations will inevitably get "older," with mean ages in the 35 to 40 range and perhaps as many as one-fourth of their members over age 60, as both mortality and fertility rates decline and human numbers (hopefully) reach stable levels. Not surprisingly, each of these aging populations will develop its own unique set of problems to resolve, not the least of which might be understandable but almost certainly misguided efforts to increase the size—and overall economic productivity—of younger age cohorts by encouraging higher fertility.

Fourth, it is important to recognize that the quantitative scale, geographic scope, escalating pace, and functional interconnectedness of these impending demographic changes are

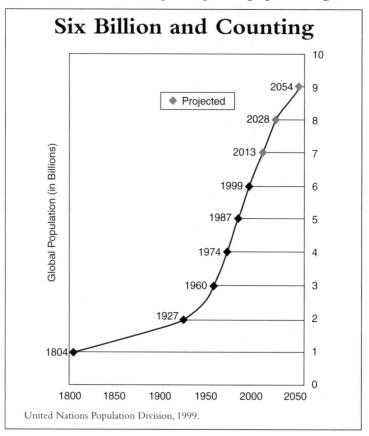

Six Billion and Counting

Global Population (in Billions)

United Nations Population Division, 1999.

of such a magnitude that there are few if any historical precedents to guide us. All previous examples of significant human population expansion—and subsequent (occasionally rapid) decline—have been primarily local or, at most, regional phenomena. At the present time, given the current global rate of increase of some 230,000 people per day (almost 10,000 per hour), it is ludicrous to speak of there being any significant empty spaces left on Earth to colonize, certainly when compared with but a century ago. And it is even more ridiculous to suggest that "off Earth" (extraterrestrial) migration will somehow be sufficient to siphon away excess human population, in either the near or more distant future.

A FINITE CARRYING CAPACITY

Fifth, given the data and observations presented thus far, it becomes increasingly apparent that the time span available for implementing an effective program of population "control" may be quite limited, with a window of opportunity—even in the more optimistic scenarios—that may not extend much beyond the middle of the [twenty-first] century. Other projections are more pessimistic, allowing no more than another 15 to 20 years for taking effective remedial action. In any event, while future population trends are notoriously difficult to predict with precision (dependent as they are on a broad range of factors), most middle-of-the-road demographic projections for the year 2040—less than two generations from now—are in the 8 to 9 billion range. . . . By any reasonable standard of comparison, this is hardly the remote future. . . . It is primarily *those already born*—ourselves, our children, and our grandchildren—who will have to confront the overwhelming impact of an additional 3 to 4 billion people within the next 40 to 50 years.

Sixth, it is extremely important to come to terms with the fact that the Earth's long-term carrying capacity, in terms of resources (broadly defined), is indeed finite, despite the continuing use of economic models predicated on seemingly unlimited growth, and notwithstanding the high probability of continued scientific/technological progress. Some further terminological clarification may be useful. "Long-term" is most reasonably defined on the order of several hundred years, at least; it emphatically does not mean the 5 to 15 year horizon typical of much economic forecasting or political prognostication. Over this much longer time span, it thus becomes much more appropriate—perhaps even essential to civilizational survival—to define a sustainable human population size in terms of optimums rather than maximums. In other words, *what "could" be supported in the short term is not necessarily what "should" be humanity's goal over the longer term.*

As far as resources are concerned, whether these be characterized as renewable or nonrenewable, it is becoming increasingly apparent that the era of inexpensive energy (derived from fossil fuels), adequate food supplies (whether plant or animal), readily available or easily extractable raw materials (from wood to minerals), plentiful fresh water, and readily accessible "open space" is rapidly coming to a close, almost certainly within the next half century. And finally, the consequences of future scientific/technological advances—whether in terms of energy production, technological efficiency, agricultural productivity, or creation of alternative materials—are much more likely to be incremental than revolutionary, notwithstanding frequent and grandiose claims for the latter.

Seventh, it is becoming increasingly apparent that rhetoric about "sustainable growth" is at best a continuing exercise in economic self-deception and at worst a politically pernicious oxymoron. Almost certainly, working toward some sort of *steady-state sustainability* is much more realistic scientifically, (probably) more attainable economically, and (perhaps) more prudent politically. Assertions that the Earth might be able to support a population of 10, 15, or even 20 billion people for an indefinite period of time at a standard of living superior to the present are not only cruelly misleading but almost certainly false. Rather, extrapolations from the work of a growing number of ecologists, demographers, and numerous others suggest the distinct possibility that *the Earth's true carrying capacity*—defined simply as humans in long-term adaptive balance with their ecological setting, resource base, and each other—*may already have been exceeded by a factor of two or more.*

To the best of my knowledge, there is no clear-cut or well-documented evidence that effectively contradicts this sobering—perhaps even frightening—assessment. Consequently, since at some point in the not-too-distant future the negative consequences and ecological damage stemming from the mutually reinforcing effects of excessive human reproduction and overconsumption of resources could well become irreversible, and because there is only one Earth with which to experiment, it is undoubtedly better for our species to err on the side of prudence, exercising wherever possible a cautious and careful stewardship.

IMPACTS ON QUALITY OF LIFE

Eighth, only about 20% of the current world population (ca. 1.2 billion people) could be said to have a *generally adequate* standard of living, defined here as a level of affluence roughly approximating that of the so-called "developed" world (Western Europe, Japan, and North America). The other 80% (ca. 4.8 billion), incorporating most of the inhabitants of what have been termed the "developing nations," live in conditions ranging from mild deprivation to severe deficiency. Despite well-intentioned efforts to the contrary, there is little evidence that this imbalance is going to decrease in any significant way, and a strong likelihood that it may get worse, particularly in view of the fact that more than 90% of all future population expansion is projected to occur in these less-developed regions of the world. In fact, there is growing concern that when this burgeoning population growth in the developing world is combined with excessive or wasteful per capita energy and resource consumption in much of the developed world, widespread environmental deterioration (systemic breakdown?) in a number of the Earth's more heavily stressed ecosystems will become increasingly likely. This is especially worrisome in regions already beset by short-sighted or counterproductive economic policies, chronic political instability, and growing social unrest, particularly when one considers that nearly all nations in the less-developed world currently have an understandable desire—not surprisingly expressed as a fundamental right—to increase their standard of living (per capita energy and resource consumption) to something approximating "first world" levels.

Ninth, to follow up on the point just made, the total impact of human numbers on the global environment is often described as the product of three basic multipliers: (1) population size; (2) per capita energy and resource consumption (affluence); and (3) technological efficiency in the production, utilization, and conservation of such energy and resources. This relationship is usually expressed by some variant of the now well-known I = PAT equation: Impact = Population × Affluence × Technology. This simple formula enables one to demonstrate much more clearly the quantitative scope of humanity's dilemma over the next 50 to 75 years, particularly if the following projections are anywhere near accurate:

- that human population could well *double* by the end of the twenty-first century, from our current 6 billion to perhaps 12 billion or more;
- that global energy and resource consumption could easily *quadruple* or more during the same period, particularly if (as just indicated in item 8) the less-developed nations are successful in their current efforts to significantly improve their citizens' standard of living to something approaching developed-world norms; and
- that "new technologies" applied to current energy and resource inefficiencies might be successful in reducing per capita waste or effluence *by half,* or even *two-thirds,* in both the developed and developing worlds.

Given these more-or-less realistic estimates, the conclusion seems inescapable that the human species' "total impact" on the Earth's already stressed ecosystem(s) could easily *triple to quadruple* by the middle of the [twenty-first] century. This impact could be even greater if current (and future) efforts at energy and resource conservation turn out to be less successful than hoped for, or if (as seems likely) the mathematical relationship between these several multipliers is something more than simply linear. It is therefore very important to keep a close watch—for harbingers of future trends and/or problems—on current events in the growing group of nations now experiencing rapid economic development and modernization, with particular attention being given to ongoing changes in India and China, two states whose combined size represents nearly half the population of the less-developed world.

FINAL CONSIDERATIONS

Tenth, and finally, there are two additional considerations—matters not usually factored into the I = PAT equation—that must also be taken into account in any attempt to coordinate appropriate responses to the rapidly increasing global environmental impact described in points 6 through 9 above. First, given current and likely ongoing scientific uncertainties about environmental limits and ecosystem resilience, not to mention the potential dangers of irreversible damage if such limits are stretched too far (i.e., a permanently reduced carrying capacity), it is extremely important to design into any future planning an adequate safety factor (or sufficient margin for error). In other words, any attempt at "guided social engineering" on the massive scale that will clearly be necessary over the next century will require at least as much attention to safety margins, internal coordination, and systems redundancy as may be found in other major engineering accomplishments—from designing airplanes to building the Channel Tunnel to landing astronauts on the moon.

In addition, such planning must consider yet another seemingly intractable problem. Because the human species not only shares the Earth—but has also co-evolved—with literally millions of other life forms, the closely related issues of wilderness conservation and biodiversity preservation must also be taken fully into account, on several different levels (pragmatic, aesthetic, and moral). In simplest terms, it has now become a matter of critical importance to ask some very basic questions about what proportion of the Earth's surface the human species has the right to exploit or transform—or, conversely, how much of the Earth's surface should be reserved for the protection and preservation of all other life forms. As many have argued, often in eloquent terms, our species will likely be more successful in confronting and resolving these questions—not to mention the other complex problems that are now crowding in upon us—if we can collectively come to regard ourselves more as the Earth's long-term stewards than its absolute masters.

To sum up, if the above "inescapable realities" are indeed valid, it is obvious that rational, equitable, and attainable population goals will have to be established in the very near future. It is also obvious that these goals will have to address—and in some fashion resolve—a powerful internal conflict: how to create and sustain an adequate standard of living for *all* the world's peoples, minimizing as much as possible the growing inequities between rich and poor, while simultaneously neither overstressing nor exceeding the Earth's longer-term carrying capacity. *I submit that these goals cannot be reached, or this conflict resolved, unless and until world population is dramatically reduced—to somewhere around two to three billion people—within the next two centuries.*

Small Is Beautiful

E.F. SCHUMACHER

E.F. Schumacher was a British civil servant whose book, *Small Is Beautiful*, became an instant best-seller in the United States and Europe. First published in 1973 it soon became a classic on economics from an environmental perspective. Schumacher argued that economic growth should reflect human need, not the perpetual drive for profits. Durable goods, that is goods that can last for many years, should be the focus of industrial production, while solar energy, conservation, and recycling would make economic life on earth sustainable. For this to happen the world needs an economic system that focuses on the dignity and sacredness of human labor. Those elements of the major faiths that promote the dignity of work and teach prudence in the stewardship of nature should be encouraged. Economics needs to be reconceptualized to prioritize the needs of all humans, including the common man.

In the excitement over the unfolding of his scientific and technical powers, modern man has built a system of production that ravishes nature and a type of society that mutilates man. If only there were more and more wealth, everything else, it is thought, would fall into place. Money is considered to be all-powerful; if it could not actually buy non-material values, such as justice, harmony, beauty or even health, it could circumvent the need for them or compensate for their loss. The development of production and the acquisition of wealth have thus become the highest goals of the modern world in relation to which all other goals, no matter how much lip-service may still be paid to them, have come to take second place. The highest goals require no justification; all secondary goals have finally to justify themselves in terms of the service their attainment renders to the attainment of the highest.

A CHALLENGE TO MATERIALISM

This is the philosophy of materialism, and it is this philosophy—or metaphysic—which is now being challenged by events. There has never been a time, in any society in any part of the world, without its sages and teachers to challenge materialism and plead for a different order of priorities. The languages have differed, the symbols have varied, yet the message has always been the same: "Seek ye *first* the kingdom of God, and all these things [the material things which you also need] shall be *added* unto you." They shall be added, we are told, here on earth where we need them, not simply in an after-life beyond our imagination. Today, however, this message reaches us not solely from the sages and saints but from the actual course of physical events. It speaks to us in the language of terrorism, genocide, breakdown, pollution, exhaustion. We live, it seems, in a unique period of convergence. It is becoming apparent that there is not only a promise but also a threat in those astonishing words about the kingdom of God—the threat that "unless you seek first the kingdom, these other things, which you also need, will cease to be available to you." As a recent writer put it, without reference to economics and politics but nonetheless with direct reference to the condition of the modern world:

> If it can be said that man collectively shrinks back more and more from the Truth, it can also be said that on all sides the Truth is closing in more and more upon man. It might almost be said that, in order to receive a touch of It, which in the past required a lifetime of effort, all that is asked of him now is not to shrink back. And yet how difficult that is!

We shrink back from the truth if we believe that the destructive forces of the modern world can be "brought under control" simply by mobilising more resources—of wealth, education, and research—to fight pollution, to preserve wildlife, to discover new sources of energy, and to arrive at more effective agreements on peaceful coexistence. Needless to say, wealth, education, research, and many other things are needed for any civilisation, but what is most needed today is a revision of the ends which these means are meant to serve. And this implies, above all else, the development of a life-style which accords to material things their proper, legitimate place, which is secondary and not primary.

The "logic of production" is neither the logic of life nor that of society. It is a small and subservient part of both. The destructive forces unleashed by it cannot be brought under control, unless the "logic of production" itself is brought under control—so that destructive forces cease to be unleashed. It is of little use trying to suppress terrorism if the production of deadly devices continues to be deemed a legitimate employment of man's creative powers. Nor can the fight against pollution be successful if the patterns of production and consumption continue to be of a scale, a complexity, and a degree of violence which, as is becoming more and more apparent, do not fit into the laws of the universe, to which man is just as much subject as the rest of creation. Equally, the chance of mitigating the rate of resource depletion or of bringing harmony into the relationships between those in possession of wealth and power and those without is non-existent as long as there is no idea anywhere of enough being good and more-than-enough being evil.

It is a hopeful sign that some awareness of these deeper issues is gradually—if exceedingly cautiously—finding expression even in some official and semi-official utterances. A report, written by a committee at the request of the Secretary of State for the Environment, talks about buying time during which technologically developed societies have an opportunity "to revise their values and to change their political objectives." It is a matter of "moral choices," says the report; "no amount of calculation can alone provide the answers. . . . The fundamental questioning of conventional values by young people all over the world is a symptom of the widespread unease with which our industrial civilisation is increasingly regarded." Pollution must be brought under control and mankind's population and consumption and sustainable equilibrium. "Unless this is done, sooner or later—and some believe that there is little time left—the downfall of civilisation will not be a matter of science fiction. It will be the experience of our children and grandchildren."

But how is it to be done? What are the "moral choices"? Is it just a matter, as the report also suggests, of deciding "how much we are willing to pay for clean surroundings"? Mankind has indeed a certain freedom of choice: it is not bound by trends, by the "logic of production," or by any other fragmentary logic. But it is bound by truth. Only in the service of truth is perfect freedom, and even those who today ask us "to free our imagination from bondage to the existing system" fail to point the way to the recognition of truth.

It is hardly likely that twentieth-century man is called upon to discover truth that has never been discovered before. In the Christian tradition, as in all genuine traditions of mankind, the truth has been stated in religious terms, a language which has become well-nigh incomprehensible to the majority of modern men. The language can be revised, and there are contemporary writers who have done so, while leaving the truth inviolate. Out of the whole Christian tradition, there is perhaps no body of teaching which is more relevant and appropriate to the modern predicament than the marvellously subtle and realistic doctrines of the Four Cardinal Virtues—*prudentia, justitia, fortitudo,* and *temperantia.*

The meaning of *prudentia,* significantly called the "mother" of all other virtues—*prudentia dicitur genitrix virtutum*—is not conveyed by the word "prudence," as currently used. It signifies the opposite of a small, mean, calculating attitude to life, which refuses to see and value anything that fails to promise an immediate utilitarian advantage.

> The pre-eminence of prudence means that realisation of the good presupposes knowledge of reality. He alone can do good who knows what things are like and what their sit-

uation is. The pre-eminence of prudence means that so-called "good intentions" and so-called "meaning well" by no means suffice. Realisation of the good presupposes that our actions are appropriate to the real situation, that is to the concrete realities which form the "environment" of a concrete human action; and that we therefore take this concrete reality seriously, with clear-eyed objectivity.

This clear-eyed objectivity, however, cannot be achieved and prudence cannot be perfected except by an attitude of "silent contemplation" of reality, during which the egocentric interests of man are at least temporarily silenced.

Only on the basis of this magnanimous kind of prudence can we achieve justice, fortitude, and *temperantia,* which means knowing when enough is enough. "Prudence implies a transformation of the knowledge of truth into decisions corresponding to reality." What, therefore, could be of greater importance today than the study and cultivation of prudence, which would almost inevitably lead to a real understanding of the three other cardinal virtues, all of which are indispensable for the survival of civilisation?

Justice relates to truth, fortitude to goodness, and *temperantia* to beauty; while prudence, in a sense, comprises all three. The type of realism which behaves as if the good, the true, and the beautiful were too vague and subjective to be adopted as the highest aims of social or individual life, or were the automatic spin-off of the successful pursuit of wealth and power, has been aptly called "crackpot-realism." Everywhere people ask: "What can I actually *do*?" The answer is as simple as it is disconcerting: we can, each of us, work to put our own inner house in order. The guidance we need for this work cannot be found in science or technology, the value of which utterly depends on the ends they serve; but it can still be found in the traditional wisdom of mankind.

Humans Must Lead Ecologically Responsible Lives

ARNE NAESS

This Norwegian philosopher and naturalist Arne Naess lent to the American environmental movement his concept of "deep ecology." Rather than preserving forests as a natural resource for future generations, or national parks for the aesthetic satisfaction they give, Naess argues that nature has intrinsic value independent of human needs or recognition. While everybody must think deeply about their place in nature they should remember that environmentalism in the traditional sense has placed too much emphasis on human values. The new emphasis on preserving nature for its own sake has percolated through the American environmental movement and is now part of the moral vision and vocabulary of many activist groups.

The international, long-range ecological movement began roughly with Rachel Carson's *Silent Spring,* over twenty years ago. By 1975, many books had come out and been read by a large audience. The Norwegian edition of *Ecology, Community, and Lifestyle* had come out in five editions. There was great public concern for our environment. But let us examine what has happened over the past twelve years.

A CHANGE IN PERSONAL LIFESTYLE

In 1975 there was a firm belief in many industrialised countries that a change in personal lifestyle might be necessary. It was on the whole quite clear what an ecologically responsible lifestyle would entail: anti-consumerism in general, with stress on low energy consumption, active support of 'self-made is well made', bicycling, collective transport, *friluftsliv,* family planning, participation in biodynamic agriculture, etc. But along a whole range of issues, defeats were many and depressing: more and more people were pressed into using private cars, the simplest and ecologically most irresponsible form of transportation. And arguments such as that stressing the small effect of low private use of energy compared to the effect of continued political support of energy-demanding industry undermined motivation. By 1980 it was not 'in' anymore to be 'ecologically minded'. Reading of ecology as a part of general education stopped practically completely. Worse: many people had the feeling that they nevertheless knew what it was all about, and did not want to hear any more distressing stories.

What will happen in the next twelve years in the realm of 'ecological' lifestyle? One positive factor is the increasing public awareness of the difference between standard of living and quality of life. A second factor: it is increasingly accepted that a large percentage of costly illnesses are caused by a harmful lifestyle. Many would disappear if we lived in an ecologically responsible manner.

Concluding that our individual lifestyle is important requires premises of a general ethical and social kind. Therefore speaking of an 'ecological lifestyle' is a tenet of the deep rather than the shallow ecological movement. Between 1975 and 1987 the deep ecological movement has gained formidably in strength, and the outlook is optimistic for further strengthening. But forces opposing the implementation of deep ecology policies have gained even more in strength, and the outlook here is also one of continuation.

One per cent increase in Gross National Product [GNP] today inflicts far greater destruction of nature than one per cent 10 or 20 years ago because it is one per cent of a far larger product. And the old rough equivalency of GNP with 'Gross National Pollution' still holds. And the efforts to increase GNP create more formidable pressures against ecological policies every year.

So significant deterioration of ecological conditions may well colour the next years in spite of the deepening of ecological consciousness. The situation has to get worse before it gets better.

The general attitude among politicians has been that if a major type of interference in the ecosystem cannot be *proven* to be bad then it is justifiable to continue with business as usual. But the concern on acid rain has increased slowly and steadily over the past decade. The warnings of one government to another not to 'export' acid rain have been until recently rather polite. It is to be expected that the tone will be harsher and that the suffering involuntary 'importers', such as the Scandinavian countries, will do more to stop their own serious sources of pollution in order to give their complaints greater weight. The outlook is dark, however, especially in regard to the export of acid rain from Eastern Europe. From the point of view of the deep ecology movement, acid rain has had the positive effect of helping people understand more clearly that to conserve forests and fisheries one has to conserve worlds of micro-organisms, soils, and systems of life which most people never noticed or cared for before. Much broader ranges of identification and wonder have been opened!

Continued deterioration of life conditions may strengthen and deepen the urge to stop acid rain production to the extent that radical political measures will be taken against the offenders. Major changes in economic, political, and ideological structures may then at last begin to unfold.

A SMALL MINORITY

Supporters of the deep ecological movement constitute a small minority, quite badly organised compared to established pressure groups. They are (sometimes for good reasons) reluctant to organise in large units. But there are lessons to be learned. Big demonstrations and other forms of large-scale, nonviolent direct action seem to work when what we try to communicate, and the way the action is done, come as a kind of surprise to the general public and cause people to stop and reflect for a moment—an increasingly difficult job, because of an increasing sense of repetition.

The years to come may see a greater emphasis on direct action directed to crucially important groups, such as politicians and heads of anti-ecological institutions. Other important groups to reach: teachers, experts, scientists, specialists in mass communication. Study of mass communication and cooperation with masters of that trade has been used to advantage by environmental groups such as Greenpeace.

The late 1970s saw cooperation between the peace movement and deep ecology. No calamity could be worse from the latter point of view than nuclear war. The arms race today supports the detrimental 'big is beautiful' trend and involves the misuse of millions of mammals in experiments with weapons, radioactivity and poisons.

Moving from the rich industrial portions of the world to the poorer majority, we find that the same type of destruction of natural systems which occurred hundreds of years ago in Europe and North America is now under way in the rest of the world, particularly Africa. But there is a major difference: in the former regions the process of destruction has been concomitant with a vast increase of wealth and standard of living, whereas in the latter this is far from the case. Thus, even the *potential* forces of wide- and long-range, responsible ecological policy are absent.

Aid from the rich is essential, but it can so easily be misused that extreme care and dedicated cooperation between institutions in both regions of the world must be at its foundation. It is important to note that the traditional cultural beliefs and practices of much of the world are favourable to the norms of the deep ecological movement.

GAINING ACCEPTANCE

The deep ecology demand for the establishment of large territories free from human development has recently gained in acceptance. It is now clear that the hundreds of millions of years of evolution of mammals and especially of large, territory-demanding animals will come to a halt if large areas of wilderness are not established and protected. Wild areas previously classified as 'voids' are now realised to be of vital importance and intrinsic value. This is an example of the kind of consciousness change that strengthens deep ecology. It must continue.

These guesses about the future of the deep ecological movement are inevitably influenced by hopes and fears. It is my hope that beings endowed with a brain like ours, developed through hundreds of millions of years in close interaction with all kinds of life will inevitably support a way of life not only narrowly favourable to this species, but favourable to the whole ecosphere in all its diversity and complexity. A uniquely endowed part of this ecosphere will not turn into its eternal enemy.

Radical Activism Can Help Protect the Environment

BILL DEVALL

Bill Devall is Professor Emeritus of Sociology at Humboldt State University in Arcata, California. He is one of the leaders of the "deep ecology" movement, whose members oppose the development of roads, bridges, and cities that destroy nature. Deep ecologists believe that nature is as important, or more important, than humans. They support any actions that prevent human civilization from encroaching on nature. In the following viewpoint, Devall writes that environmental activists are justified in damaging logging equipment, pulling up survey stakes, and sinking fishing vessels to protect the environment. Devall equates these activists with the followers of Mohandas Gandhi and Martin Luther King Jr., who used civil disobedience to achieve social justice.

A small group of men and women kneel in front of an advancing bulldozer on a road being built by the U.S. Forest Service on Bald Mountain in the Kalmiopsis wilderness of southwestern Oregon. They have made repeated appeals to U.S. Forest Service officials to abandon their plans to build this road into a pristine forest area. They are now engaged in a nonviolent protest against the destruction of an incredibly wild and biologically diverse area.

In San Francisco, lawyers for Native American and environmental groups go to the federal courthouse to file for an injunction against the Forest Service. They are seeking to prevent the government from building a road through the sacred high country of the Siskiyou Mountains in northwestern California.

POLITICAL ACTIVISM

At Fishing Bridge in Yellowstone National Park, protesters dressed in bear costumes pass out leaflets to visitors. The protesters are denouncing the destruction of grizzly bear habitat by the National Park Service and calling on the agency to engage in a different kind of policy—managing visitors to the park rather than managing bears by killing ones that cause "problems."

Since 1984, many people who eat beef objected to using beef from Latin America, raised on pasture lands which had previously been rain forests. This beef was imported to the U.S.A. and used by some fast food restaurants. Boycotts and protests at some of these restaurants by concerned environmental activists led at least one company to decide against further purchases of the beef.

These are just a few of the types of action which are labeled *political activism* in the environmental movement. The deep, long-range ecology movement is only partly a political movement. Political activism, however, is one way of demonstrating solidarity with our bioregion, with some other species of plants or animals, and solidarity with each other in the movement. We set limits on corporations and governments by our activism and at the same time affirm the integrity of places close to our hearts.

Grassroots activism is a basic thrust of the Green movements, bioregional movements, restoration movements, and environmental movements such as Earth First! Grassroots environmental movements are based on the principles of nonviolence and direct action.

NONVIOLENT DIRECT ACTION

"They have the power," I'm told. "What can I do that will matter? They can do anything they want."

"They"—the military, economic elites, corporations—do

have a certain type of power that should be acknowledged. But we are not trapped in their type of power. The problem is this: by accepting theirs as the only legitimate source of power, we deny our own. When we say we can't do anything important we usually mean we can't see how we can achieve our goals. We get stuck on the goal and not the process.

Empowering ourselves means recognizing and acting from our own source of power. Right action includes words, acts and feelings true to our intuitions and principles.

For some people this means living our daily lives in a simple but rich and full way—saying grace at meals, growing a garden, riding a bicycle to work. Others may participate in nonviolent direct action; Greenpeace, the international environmental group, has engaged in many nonviolent campaigns. In Australia, in the late 1970s, activists protesting proposed dams on the Franklin River of Tasmania staged effective nonviolent protests over many months. Anyone contemplating this type of direct action can learn many lessons from reading the history of the Tasmanian wilderness campaign. . . .

Direct action in the ecology movement is one way to generate tension, to expose myths and assumptions of the dominant mindset, to create a situation in which corporations, developers and government agents are willing to negotiate. The activist is saying, "We seek negotiations. We are not interested in vandalism or terrorism. We are not seeking vengeance nor threatening the safety of citizens." Disabling a bulldozer which is posed to invade habitat of an endangered species is an act of resistance, not vandalism. Standing between seals and seal hunters is an act of resistance—creating tension—not an attack on sealers. . . .

SEA SHEPHERDS

In November 1986 under the cover of early winter darkness, two volunteers working with the Sea Shepherd Conservation Society entered two boats used by the Icelandic whaling industry in Reykjavik Harbor. The volunteers sent the vessels to the bottom of the harbor by opening the seacocks and flooding the engine rooms. They also considered sinking a third ship but found a night watchman aboard (the Sea Shepherd Society has pledged it will not injure any person in its protest actions). During the same action, they sabotaged the whale processing plant in Reykjavik Harbor and destroyed the computer room of the Icelandic whaling industry.

Rod Coronado, the young man who planned and executed the raid on Reykjavik, is a defender of whales who agreed to follow the Sea Shepherd Society guidelines for action in the field: no explosives; no weapons; no action that has even a remote possibility of causing injury to a living being; if apprehended, do not resist arrest in a violent manner; be prepared to accept full responsibility and suffer the possible consequences of your actions.

Paul Watson, spokesperson for the Sea Shepherd Society, declared that the action "was done to strike a blow against the whaling industry." Iceland had continued to defy decisions from the International Whaling Commission concerning the number and type of whales that could be harpooned annually.

The action against the Icelandic whaling fleet was not the first by the Sea Shepherd Society against illegal whaling. In 1979 the *Sea Shepherd* rammed a "pirate" whaling vessel, the *Sierra,* off the coast of Portugal. Both vessels were towed to the Portuguese port of Leixoes and the *Sea Shepherd* was later confiscated. Paul Watson and the two other crew members who remained on board during the ramming escaped from the country. Volunteers later went back to Portugal to attach a magnetic mine to the hull of the *Sierra.* It sank quickly.

UNCONVENTIONAL DEFENSE

The Sea Shepherd Society is not alone in taking unconventional action in defense of animals. Under the banner of animal liberation, small groups have invaded laboratories of colleges and universities to liberate primates and other animals used in experiments. In 1985 in Hawaii two dolphins were liberated from captivity.

Protests against certain logging practices have occurred in

Australia, Oregon, Texas, California, and other areas. Protesters, chaining themselves to bulldozers or climbing trees, have refused to disperse when ordered by police and have been arrested. In the Solomon Islands in the South Pacific, villagers attacked and burned the logging camp and equipment owned by a multinational corporation which had been granted a timber lease to the island by the central government.

Actions such as these have been aggressively reported by the news media. Some groups, such as Greenpeace, have actively sought publicity for their nonviolent encounters with the Russian whaling fleet and with officials of the French government. In 1985, instead of stopping their nuclear weapons testing in the South Pacific, the French government tried to stop Greenpeace protests. In that instance the Greenpeace vessel *Rainbow Warrior* was being outfitted in an Auckland, New Zealand, harbor in preparation for a voyage into the French nuclear test zone in the South Pacific. On orders from officials at the top level of the French government, agents of the French intelligence agency entered New Zealand on false passports and attached a bomb to the Greenpeace vessel. The explosion sent the *Rainbow Warrior* to the bottom of Auckland Harbor and killed a crew member, Fernando Pereira, who was preparing to sail with Greenpeace into the French nuclear test zone. The *Rainbow Warrior* was refloated but could not be restored to seaworthy status. It was towed into the South Pacific and sunk.

For over a hundred years the conservation-environmental movement was remarkably resistant to use of protest demonstrations or direct action as tactics in campaigns. From the days of John Muir, environmentalists relied on letter writing campaigns, appeals to elected officials, and publicity campaigns to arouse the sympathy of the public for an endangered area. In comparison to other movements of equal vigor, such as the labor movement, the environmental movement has been remarkably free from violence and street demonstrations.

Thoreau in his famous essay "On Civil Disobedience," written after he spent the night in jail for refusing to pay a tax levied to support the War in Mexico in 1845, provided strong defense for the moral claims of civil disobedience when one is acting from deeply held convictions. Gandhi and Martin Luther King, Jr. greatly developed strategies and philosophies for civil disobedience campaigns. In the later part of the twentieth century, grassroots environmental movements have begun to use civil disobedience. To better understand these campaigns, it is necessary to define some phrases which some politicians and news media have been using disparagingly.

Direct action is action taken in defense of a forest, river, or specific species of plants or animals, in which the protester has no monetary or private property interest, but has a concern as part of his or her ecological self and makes a statement with his or her body. To paraphrase Gandhi: I serve no one but myself, but my *self* is broad and deep. A protest march in front of a U.S. Forest Service [office] or blocking public access to roads leading to a logging site is direct action when the protesters are attempting to call attention to the integrity of a primeval forest. Sailing a vessel into an area of ocean decreed by a government as a "prohibited zone" to protest government policies is direct action. So is sitting in a small boat between whales and whalers' harpoons.

Monkeywrenching is the purposeful dismantling or disabling of artifacts used in environmentally destructive practices at a specific site—dismantling fishing gear or logging equipment, for example.

Ecotage is disabling a technological or bureaucratic operation in defense of one's place. It is self-defense. According to the dictionary, ecotage is a combination of ecology and sabotage. Ecology comes from combining the Greek *oikos*, a household, and *logy*, to study; *saboter* means to damage machinery with wooden shoes. Ecotage, as used there, means actions which can be executed without injury to life.

Sam Lovejoy, who engaged in antinuclear ecotage in New England, wrote that ecotage is directed, targeted, and ethical action in defense of living systems. It is not action which could be considered vandalism or random attacks on technology....

POWERFUL ACTIONS

Monkeywrenching and ecotage are powerful (and personally empowering) actions which require the participant to "step outside of the system," in the words of Dave Foreman, and take responsibility for defending a piece of territory to protect its integrity. "Maybe it [monkeywrenching] is not going to stop everything. Maybe it's not going to change the world, but it's going to buy that place, those creatures, some time. And maybe that's the best that can be done."

Monkeywrenching calls us to a place in our own minds that we have perhaps not visited before, a place of alertness, attention, perception to the whole situation. Foreman's book, *Ecodefense,* is concerned primarily with what he calls "strategic monkeywrenching," which he says is thoughtful, deliberate and safe for participants and other people who might be in the area.

Strategic monkeywrenching is used only when attempting to protect areas which are not legally protected as wilderness but have great beauty, biological diversity, integrity of place and wilderness, and are threatened by some specific action such as road construction, natural resource exploration or energy developments.

According to Foreman, strategic monkeywrenching is based on the following principles:

1. It is nonviolent. "It is not directed towards harming human beings or other forms of life."

2. It is not organized by a formal group. "It is truly individual action."

3. It may be a project of a small affinity group.

4. It is targeted. The focus of activity is specific; for example, stopping or delaying destruction in a specific area as part of a larger strategy to obtain official protection.

5. It is timely. It has a proper place in the total campaign. Monkeywrenchers make a clear and accurate assessment of the political situation.

6. It is dispersed. There is no central clearinghouse of information on monkeywrenching. No records are kept of operations.

7. It is diverse. Many kinds of people are involved. It is nonelitist. It is *not* paramilitary action.

8. It is fun. "There is a rush of excitement." It can also be very dangerous.

9. It is *not* revolutionary. "It does not aim to overthrow any social, political or economic system. It is merely nonviolent self-defense of the wild."

10. It is simple. "Use the simplest tool and method."

11. It is deliberate and ethical, *not* vandalistic or unpremeditated. "They keep a pure heart and mind about it. They remember that they are engaged in the most moral of all actions: protecting life, defending the Earth."

PUBLIC AWARENESS AND PERSONAL RISK

Animal rights or animal liberation advocates used strategic monkeywrenching and ecotage to rescue hundreds of laboratory animals from cruel and painful experiments. Widespread publicity concerning their actions has aroused a storm of discussion concerning ethical responsibilities of scientists and students toward these animals. Furthermore, the discussion has extended to other facilities such as zoos, fur companies, slaughterhouse operations, and cosmetic corporations using animals to test chemicals. The ripple effect has led to widespread public awareness of behavior that was considered "usual" or "ordinary." Ecotage and monkeywrenching tactics used by animal rights advocates helped unveil some of the assumptions of the dominant society and led to constructive dialogue.

Specific techniques of monkeywrenching and ecotage are discussed at length in Foreman's book and in the "Ned Ludd" column of the *Earth First!* journal. Techniques should be selected after considering moral and technical factors and the competency of the persons taking part.

I see an analogy between rescuers of Jews and homosexuals in Nazi-occupied Europe and strategic monkeywrenching in the late twentieth century. As part of Dr. Samuel Oliner's academic study of helping behavior during the Holocaust, he interviewed a sample of people who had been rescued, some

of the rescuers, as well as people living in the same area as rescuers who did not risk themselves to help victims. Oliner
found a number of similarities among rescuers, including an
openness of character, willingness to take risks, spontaneity in
the desperate situation, personalizing the situation through em-
pathy with victims, and creativity. He collected many stories
of ordinary people who, in extraordinary situations, found
ways to help another person not of their own race or religion.
These same traits can be applied to practitioners of deep ecology, who are, in a sense, rescuers of the environment.

Government Intervention Can Help the Environment

AL GORE JR.

At the time he wrote the following viewpoint, Al Gore Jr. was a U.S. Senator from Tennessee. Gore contends that the federal government has a role to play in saving the environment by committing diverse agencies to coordinate in developing a comprehensive environmental policy. Gore suggests that significant federal spending is needed to address such environmental problems as global warming, ozone depletion, deforestation, and various forms of pollution.

How can we possibly explain the mistakes and false starts President Bush has been making on environmental policy? His administration's decision to censor scientific testimony on the seriousness of the greenhouse effect—and initially to oppose an international convention to begin working out a solution to it—may well mean that the president himself does not yet see the threat clearly. Apparently he does not hear the alarms that are awakening so many other leaders from Margaret Thatcher to Mikhail Gorbachev.

Humankind has suddenly entered into a brand new relationship with the planet Earth. The world's forests are being destroyed; an enormous hole is opening in the ozone layer. Living species are dying at an unprecedented rate. Chemical wastes, in growing volumes, are seeping downward to poison groundwater while huge quantities of carbon dioxide, methane

Excerpted from "We Need a Strategic Initiative for the Environment," by Al Gore Jr., *Washington Post National Weekly Edition*, May 22–28, 1989. Copyright © 1989 by The Washington Post. Reprinted with permission.

and chlorofluorocarbons are trapping heat in the atmosphere and raising global temperatures.

How much information is needed to recognize a pattern? How much more is needed by the body politic to justify action in response?

If an individual or a nation is accustomed to looking at the future one year at a time, and the past in terms of a single lifetime, then many large patterns are concealed. But seen in historical perspective, it is clear that dozens of destructive effects have followed the same pattern of unprecedented acceleration in the latter half of the 20th century. It took 10,000 human lifetimes for the population to reach two billion. Now in the course of one lifetime, yours and mine, it is rocketing from two to 10 billion, and is already halfway there.

Yet, the pattern of our politics remains remarkably unchanged. That indifference must end. As a nation and a government, we must see that America's future is inextricably tied to the fate of the globe. In effect, the environment is becoming a matter of national security—an issue that directly and imminently menaces the interests of the state or the welfare of the people. . . .

However, it is important to distinguish what would—in military jargon—be called the level of threat. Certain environmental problems may be important but are essentially local; others cross borders, and in effect represent theaters of operations; still others are global and strategic. On this scale, the slow suffocation of Mexico City, the deaths of forests in America and Europe or even the desertification of large areas of Africa might not be regarded as full-scale national security issues. But the greenhouse effect and stratospheric ozone depletion *do* fit the profile of strategic national security issues.

RADICAL RESPONSES

When nations perceive that they are threatened at the strategic level, they may be induced to think of drastic responses, involving sharp discontinuities from everyday approaches to policy. In military terms, this is the point when the United States begins to think of invoking nuclear weapons. The global environmental crisis may demand responses that are equally radical.

At present, despite some progress made toward limiting some sources of the problem, such as chlorofluorocarbons (CFCs), we have barely scratched the surface. Even if all other elements of the problem are solved, a major threat is still posed by emissions of carbon dioxide, the exhaling breath of the industrial culture upon which our civilization rests. The implications of the latest and best studies on this matter are staggering. Essentially, they tell us that with our current pattern of technology and production, we face a choice between economic growth in the near term and massive environmental disorder as the subsequent penalty.

This central fact suggests that the notion of environmentally sustainable development at present may be an oxymoron, rather than a realistic objective. It declares war, in effect, on routine life in the advanced industrial societies. And—central to the outcome of the entire struggle to restore global environmental balance—it declares war on the Third World.

If the Third World does not develop economically, poverty, hunger and disease will consume entire populations. Rapid economic growth is a life-or-death imperative. And why should they accept what we, manifestly, will not accept for ourselves? Will any nation in the developed world accept serious compromises in levels of comfort for the sake of global environmental balance? Who will apportion these sacrifices; who will bear them?

The effort to solve the nuclear arms race has been complicated not only by simplistic stereotypes of the enemy and the threat he poses, but by simplistic demands for immediate unilateral disarmament.

Similarly, the effort to solve the global environmental crisis will be complicated not only by blind assertions that more environmental manipulation and more resource extraction are essential for economic growth. It will also be complicated by the emergence of simplistic demands that development, or technology itself, must be stopped for the problem to be solved. This is a crisis of confidence which must be addressed.

The tension between the imperatives of growth and the imperative of environmental management represents a supreme test for modern industrial civilization and an extreme demand upon technology. It will call for the environmental equivalent of the Strategic Defense Initiative: a Strategic Environment Initiative [SEI]. . . .

We need the same kind of focus and intensity, and similar levels of funding, to deal comprehensively with global warming, stratospheric ozone depletion, species loss, deforestation, ocean pollution, acid rain, air and water and groundwater pollution. In every major sector of economic activity a Strategic Environment Initiative must identify and then spread increasingly effective new technologies: some that are already in hand; some that need further work; and some that are revolutionary ideas whose very existence is now a matter of speculation.

For example, energy is the life blood of development. Unfortunately, today's most economical technologies for converting energy resources into useable forms of power (such as burning coal to make electricity) release a plethora of pollutants. An Energy SEI should focus on producing energy for development without compromising the environment. Priorities for the near term are efficiency and conservation; for the mid-term, solar power, possibly new-generation nuclear power, and biomass sources (with no extraneous pollutants and a closed carbon cycle); and for the long term, nuclear fusion, as well as enhanced versions of developing technologies.

In agriculture, we have witnessed vast growth in Third World food production through the Green Revolution, but often that growth relied on heavily subsidized fertilizers, pesticides, irrigation and mechanization, sometimes giving the advantage to rich farmers over poor ones. We need a second green revolution, to address the needs of the Third World's poor: a focus on increasing productivity from small farms on marginal land with low-input agricultural methods. These technologies, which include financial and political components, may be the key to satisfying the land hunger of the disadvantaged and the desperate who are slashing daily into the rain forest of Amazonia. It may also be the key to arresting the desertification of Sub-Saharan Africa, where human need and climate stress now operate in a deadly partnership.

Needed in the United States probably more than anywhere is a Transportation SEI focusing in the near term on improving the mileage standards of our vehicles, and encouraging and enabling Americans to drive less. In the mid-term come questions of alternative fuels, such as biomass-based liquids or electricity.

THE TRANSPORTATION SECTOR

Later will come the inescapable need for reexamining the entire structure of our transportation sector, with its inherent emphasis on the personal vehicle. The U.S. government should organize itself to finance the export of energy-efficient systems and renewable energy sources. That means preferential lending arrangements through the Export-Import Bank of the United States and the Overseas Private Investment Corp.

Encouragement for the Third World should also come in the form of attractive international credit arrangements for energy-efficient and environmentally sustainable processes. Funds could be generated by institutions such as the World Bank, which, in the course of debt swapping, might dedicate new funds to the purchase of more environmentally sound technologies.

Finally, the United States, other developers of new technology and international lending institutions should establish centers of training at locations around the world to create a core of environmentally educated planners and technicians—an effort not unlike that which produced agricultural research centers during the Green Revolution.

Immediately, we should undertake an urgent effort to obtain massive quantities of information about the global processes now underway—through, for example, the Mission to Planet Earth program of NASA [National Aeronautics and Space Administration].

And we also must target first the most readily identifiable and correctable sources of environmental damage. I have introduced a comprehensive legislative package that incorporates the major elements of this SEI: It calls for a ban, within five years, on CFCs and other ozone-depleting chemicals, while promoting development of safer alternatives; radically reducing carbon dioxide emissions and increasing fuel efficiency; encouraging massive reforestation programs; and initiating comprehensive recycling efforts.

Although Congress is recognizing the challenge, there remains a critical need for presidential leadership, for President Bush to show that as a nation we have the vision and the courage to act responsibly. And in order to accomplish our goal, we also must transform global politics, shifting from short-term concerns to long-term goals, from conflict to cooperation. But we must also transform ourselves—or at least the way we think about ourselves, our children and our future. The solutions we seek will be found in a new faith in the future of life on earth after our own, a faith in the future that justifies sacrifices in the present, a new moral courage to choose higher values in the conduct of human affairs, and a new reverence for absolute principles that can serve as guiding stars for the future course of our species and our place within creation.

CHAPTER 5

NARRATIVES

AMERICAN
SOCIAL
MOVEMENTS

America Needs a National Park

GEORGE CATLIN

This proposal, written by artist and anthropologist George Catlin, may be the first call for a national park in American history. Catlin worries that wild lands and animals that inhabit them will disappear. Living among Native American tribes Catlin learned their languages, sketched profusely, and prepared for publication a book titled The North American Portfolio in 1844. His paintings deeply affected Americans and Europeans alike, and now hang in the Catlin gallery in the National Museum, Washington, D.C.

When I first arrived at this place, on my way up the river, which was in the month of May, in 1832, and had taken up my lodgings in the Fur Company's Fort, . . . [I was told] that only a few days before I arrived (when an immense herd of buffaloes had showed themselves on the opposite side of the river, almost blackening the plains for a great distance), a party of five or six hundred Sioux Indians on horseback, forded the river about mid-day, and spending a few hours amongst them, recrossed the river at sun-down and came into the Fort with *fourteen hundred fresh buffalo tongues,* which were thrown down in a mass, and for which they required but a few gallons of whiskey, which was soon demolished, indulging them in a little, and harmless carouse.

This profligate waste of the lives of these noble and useful animals, when, from all that I could learn, not a skin or a pound of the meat (except the tongues), was brought in, fully supports me in the seemingly extravagant predictions that I have made as to their extinction, which I am certain is near at hand. . . .

Excerpted from vol. 1 of *North American Indians; Being Letters and Notes on Their Manners, Customs, and Conditions, Written During Eight Years' Travel Amongst the Wildest Tribes of Indians in North America, 1832–1839,* 2 vols., by George Catlin (Philadelphia: Leary, Stuart, 1913).

From the above remarks it will be seen, that not only the red men, but red men and white, have aimed destruction at the race of these animals. . . .

Thus much I wrote of the buffaloes, and . . . of the fate that awaits them; and before I closed my book [i.e., diary or journal], I strolled out one day to the shade of a plum-tree, where I lay in the grass on a favourite bluff, and wrote thus:—

It is generally supposed, and familiarly said that a man *'falls'* into a rêverie; but I seated myself in the shade a few minutes since, resolved to *force* myself into one; and for this purpose I laid open a small pocket-map of North America, and excluding my thoughts from every other object in the world, I soon succeeded in producing the desired illusion. This little chart, over which I bent, was seen in all its parts, as nothing but the green and vivid reality. I was lifted up upon an imaginary pair of wings, which easily raised and held me floating in the open air, from whence I could behold beneath me the Pacific and the Atlantic Oceans—the great cities of the East, and the mighty rivers. I could see the blue chain of the great lakes at the North—the Rocky Mountains, and beneath them and near their base, the vast, and almost boundless plains of grass, which were speckled with the bands of grazing buffaloes!

The world turned gently around, and I examined its surface; continent after continent passed under my eye, and yet amidst them all, I saw not the vast and vivid green, that is spread like a carpet over the Western wilds of my own country. I saw not elsewhere in the world, the myriad herds of buffaloes—my eyes scanned in vain for they were not. And when I turned again to the wilds of my native land, I beheld them all in motion! For the distance of several hundreds of miles from North to South, they were wheeling about in vast columns and herds—some were scattered, and ran with furious wildness—some lay dead, and others were pawing the earth for a hiding-place—some were sinking down and dying, gushing out their life's blood in deep-drawn sighs—and others were contending in furious battle for the life they possessed, and the ground that they stood upon. They had long since assembled from the thickets, and secret haunts of the deep forest, into the midst of the treeless and bushless plains, as the place for their safety. I could see in an hundred places, amid the wheeling bands, and, on their skirts and flanks, the leaping wild horse darting among them. I saw not the arrows, nor heard the twang of the sinewy bows that sent them; but I saw their victims fall!—on other steeds that rushed along their sides, I saw the glistening lances, which seemed to lay across them; their blades were blazing in the sun, till dipped in blood, and then I lost them! In other parts (and there were many), the vivid flash of *fire-arms* was seen—*their* victims fell too, and over their dead bodies hung suspended in air, little clouds of whitened smoke, from under which the flying horsemen had darted forward to mingle again with, and deal death to, the trampling throng.

. . . Hundreds and thousands were strewed upon the plains—they were flayed, and their reddened carcasses left; and about them bands of wolves, and dogs, and buzzards were seen devouring them. Contiguous, and in sight, were the distant and feeble smokes of wigwams and villages, where the skins were dragged, and dressed for white man's luxury! where they were all sold for *whiskey,* and the poor Indians lay drunk, and were

The buffalo population plummeted as Native Americans and European settlers overhunted herds and significantly limited their habitats.

crying. I cast my eyes into the towns and cities of the East, and there I beheld buffalo robes hanging at almost every door for traffic; and I saw also the curling smokes of a thousand *Stills*— and I said, 'Oh insatiable man, is thy avarice such! wouldst thou tear the skin from the back of the last animal of this noble race, *and rob thy fellow-man of his meat, and for it give him poison!'*

Many are the rudenesses and wilds in Nature's works, which are destined to fall before the deadly axe and desolating hands of cultivating man; and so amongst her ranks of *living,* of beast and human, we often find noble stamps, or beautiful colours, to which our admiration clings; and even in the overwhelming march of civilised improvements and refinements do we love to cherish their existence, and lend our efforts to preserve them in their primitive rudeness. Such of Nature's works are always worthy of our preservation and protection; and the further we become separated (and the face of the country) from that pristine wildness and beauty, the more pleasure does the mind of enlightened man feel in recurring to those scenes, when he can have them preserved for his eyes and his mind to dwell upon.

Of such "rudenesses and wilds," Nature has nowhere presented more beautiful and lovely scenes, than those of the vast prairies of the West; and of *man* and *beast,* no nobler specimens than those who inhabit them—the *Indian* and the *buffalo*— joint and original tenants of the soil, and fugitives together from the approach of civilised man; they have fled to the great plains of the West, and there, under an equal doom, they have taken up their *last abode,* where their race will expire, and their bones will bleach together.

It may be that *power is right,* and *voracity a virtue;* and that these people, and these noble animals, are *righteously* doomed to an issue that *will* not be averted. It can be easily proved— we have a civilised science that can easily do it, or anything else that may be required to cover the iniquities of civilised man in catering for his unholy appetites. It can be proved that the weak and ignorant have no *rights*—that there can be no virtue in darkness—that God's gifts have no meaning or merit until they are appropriated by civilised man—by him brought into the light, and converted to his use and luxury. . . .

Reader! Listen to the following calculations, and forget them not. The buffaloes (the quadrupeds from whose backs your beautiful robes were taken, and whose myriads were once spread over the whole country, from the Rocky Mountains to the Atlantic Ocean) have recently fled before the appalling appearance of civilised man, and taken up their abode and pasturage amid the almost boundless prairies of the West. An instinctive dread of their deadly foes, who made an easy prey of them whilst grazing in the forest, has led them to seek the midst of the vast and treeless plains of grass, as the spot where they would be least exposed to the assaults of their enemies; and it is exclusively in those desolate fields of silence (yet of beauty) that they are to be found—and over these vast steppes, or prairies, have they fled, like the Indian, towards the "setting sun;" until their bands have been crowded together, and their limits confined to a narrow strip of country on this side of the Rocky Mountains.

This strip of country, which extends from the province of Mexico to Lake Winnipeg on the North, is almost one entire plain of grass, which is, and ever must be, useless to cultivating man. It is here, and here chiefly, that the buffaloes dwell; and with, and hovering about them, live and flourish the tribes of Indians, whom God made for the enjoyment of that fair land and its luxuries.

It is a melancholy contemplation for one who has travelled as I have, through these realms, and seen this noble animal in all its pride and glory, to contemplate it so rapidly wasting from the world, drawing the irresistible conclusion too, which one must do, that its species is soon to be extinguished, and with it the peace and happiness (if not the actual existence) of the tribes of Indians who are joint tenants with them, in the occupancy of these vast and idle plains.

And what a splendid contemplation too, when one (who has travelled these realms, and can duly appreciate them) imagines them as they *might* in future be seen (by some great protecting policy of government) preserved in their pristine beauty and wildness, in a *magnificent park,* where the world could see for ages to come, the native Indian in his classic attire, galloping his wild horse, with sinewy bow, and shield and lance, amid the fleeting herds of elks and buffaloes. What a beautiful and thrilling specimen for America to preserve and hold up to the view of her refined citizens and the world, in future ages! A *nation's Park,* containing man and beast, in all the wild and freshness of their nature's beauty!

I would ask no other monument to my memory, nor any other enrolment of my name amongst the famous dead, than the reputation of having been the founder of such an institution.

Living on Walden Pond

HENRY DAVID THOREAU

American writer Henry David Thoreau left the small town of Concord, Massachusetts, to live for part of the year by Walden Pond and observe nature first hand. His observations became a classic work in American literature and have inspired many to attempt a closer relationship with the natural world. In *Walden* he lovingly describes the workings of nature in its many seasons at Walden Pond, and in philosophical musings contrasts a life lived close to nature to one lived in the town. Thoreau's work inspired many readers to preserve and set aside land so that the spiritual regeneration and wellness that accompany time spent in nature can flourish.

Sometimes having had a surfeit of human society and gossip, and worn out all my village friends, I rambled still farther westward than I habitually dwell, into yet more unfrequented parts of the town, "to fresh woods and pastures new," or, while the sun was setting, made my supper of huckleberries and blueberries on Fair Haven Hill, and laid up a store for several days. The fruits do not yield their true flavor to the purchaser of them, nor to him who raises them for the market. There is but one way to obtain it, yet few take that way. If you would know the flavor of huckleberries, ask the cow-boy or the partridge. It is a vulgar error to suppose that you have tasted huckleberries who never plucked them. A huckleberry never reaches Boston; they have not been known there since they grew on her three hills. The ambrosial and essential part of the fruit is lost with the bloom which is rubbed off in the market cart, and they become mere provender. As long as

Excerpted from *Walden*, by Henry David Thoreau (1854).

Eternal Justice reigns, not one innocent huckleberry can be transported thither from the country's hills.

Occasionally, after my hoeing was done for the day, I joined some impatient companion who had been fishing on the pond since morning, as silent and motionless as a duck or a floating leaf, and, after practising various kinds of philosophy, had concluded commonly, by the time I arrived, that he belonged to the ancient sect of Coenobites. There was one older man, an excellent fisher and skilled in all kinds of woodcraft, who was pleased to look upon my house as a building erected for the convenience of fishermen; and I was equally pleased when he sat in my doorway to arrange his lines. Once in a while we sat together on the pond, he at one end of the boat, and I at the other; but not many words passed between us, for he had grown deaf in his later years, but he occasionally hummed a psalm, which harmonized well enough with my philosophy. Our intercourse was thus altogether one of unbroken harmony far more pleasing to remember than if it had been carried on by speech. When, as was commonly the case, I had none to commune with, I used to raise the echoes by striking with a paddle on the side of my boat, filling the surrounding woods with circling and dilating sound, stirring them up as the keeper of a menagerie his wild beasts, until I elicited a growl from every wooded vale and hill-side.

In warm evenings I frequently sat in the boat playing the flute, and saw the perch, which I seem to have charmed, hovering around me, and the moon travelling over the ribbed bottom, which was strewed with the wrecks of the forest. Formerly I had come to this pond adventurously, from time to time, in dark summer nights, with a companion, and making a fire close to the water's edge, which we thought attracted the fishes, we caught pouts with a bunch of worms strung on a thread, and when we had done, far in the night, threw the burning brands high in the air like skyrockets, which, coming down into the pond, were quenched with a loud hissing, and we were suddenly groping in total darkness. Through this, whistling a tune, we took our way to the haunts of men again.

But now I had made my home by the shore.

Sometimes, after staying in a village parlor till the family had all retired, I have returned to the woods, and, partly with a view to the next day's dinner, spent the hours of midnight fishing from a boat by moonlight, serenaded by owls and foxes, and hearing, from time to time, the creaking note of some unknown bird close at hand. These experiences were very memorable and valuable to me,—anchored in forty feet of water, and twenty or thirty rods from the shore, surrounded sometimes by thousands of small perch and shiners, dimpling the surface with their tails in the moonlight, and communicating by a long flaxen line with mysterious nocturnal fishes which had their dwelling forty feet below, or sometimes dragging sixty feet of line about the pond as I drifted in the gentle night breeze, now and then feeling a slight vibration along it, indicative of some life prowling about its extremity, of dull uncertain blundering purpose there, and slow to make up its mind. At length you slowly raise, pulling hand over hand, some horned pout squeaking and squirming to the upper air. It was very queer, especially in dark nights, when your thoughts had wandered to vast and cosmogonal themes in other spheres, to feel this faint jerk, which came to interrupt your dreams and link you to Nature again. It seemed as if I might next cast my line upward into the air, as well as downward into this element, which was scarcely more dense. Thus I caught two fishes as it were with one hook.

The scenery of Walden is on a humble scale, and, though very beautiful, does not approach to grandeur, nor can it much concern one who has not long frequented it or lived by its shore; yet this pond is so remarkable for its depth and purity as to merit a particular description. It is a clear and deep green well, half a mile long and a mile and three quarters in circumference, and contains about sixty-one and a half acres; a perennial spring in the midst of pine and oak woods, without any visible inlet or outlet except by the clouds and evaporation. The surrounding hills rise abruptly from the water to the height of forty to eighty feet, though on the south-east and east they attain to about one hundred and one hundred and fifty feet respectively, within a quarter and a third of a mile. They are exlusively woodland. All our Concord waters have two colors at least; one when viewed at a distance, and another, more proper, close at hand. The first depends more on the light, and follows the sky. In clear weather, in summer, they appear blue at a little distance, especially if agitated, and at a great distance all appear alike. In stormy weather they are sometimes of a dark slate color. The sea, however, is said to be blue one day and green another without any perceptible change in the atmosphere. I have seen our river, when, the landscape being covered with snow, both water and ice were almost as green as grass. Some consider blue "to be the color of pure water, whether liquid or solid." But, looking directly down into our waters from a boat, they are seen to be of very different colors. Walden is blue at one time and green at another, even from the same point of view. Lying between the earth and the heavens, it partakes of the color of both. Viewed from a hill-top it reflects the color of the sky; but near at hand it is of a yellowish tint next the shore where you can see the sand, then a light green, which gradually deepens to a uniform dark green in the body of the pond. In some lights, viewed even from a hill-top, it is of a vivid green next the shore. Some have referred this to the reflection of the verdure; but it is equally green there against the railroad sand-bank, and in the spring, before the leaves are expanded, and it may be simply the result of the prevailing blue mixed with the yellow of the sand. Such is the color of its iris. This is that portion also, where in the spring, the ice being warmed by the heat of the sun reflected from the bottom, and also transmitted through the earth, melts first and forms a narrow canal about the still frozen middle. Like the rest of our waters, when much agitated, in clear weather, so that the surface of the waves may reflect the sky at the right angle, or because there is more light mixed with it, it appears at a little distance of a darker blue than the sky itself; and at such a time, being on its surface, and looking with divided vision, so as to see the reflection, I have discerned a matchless and indescribable light blue, such as watered or changeable silks and sword blades suggest, more cerulean than the sky itself, alternating with the original dark green on the opposite sides of the waves, which last appeared but muddy in comparison. It is a vitreous greenish blue, as I remember it, like those patches of the winter sky seen through cloud vistas in the west before sundown. Yet a single glass of its water held up to the light is as colorless as an equal quantity of air. It is well known that a large plate of glass will have a green tint, owing, as the makers say, to its "body," but a small piece of the same will be colorless. How large a body of Walden water would be required to reflect a green tint I have never proved. The water of our river is black or a very dark brown to one looking directly down on it, and, like that of most ponds, imparts to the body of one bathing in it a yellowish tinge; but this water is of such crystalline purity that the body of the bather appears of an alabaster whiteness, still more unnatural, which, as the limbs are magnified and distorted withal, produces a monstrous effect, making fit studies for a Michael Angelo.

The water is so transparent that the bottom can easily be discerned at the depth of twenty-five or thirty feet. Paddling over it, you may see many feet beneath the surface the schools of perch and shiners, perhaps only an inch long, yet the former easily distinguished by their transverse bars, and you think that they must be ascetic fish that find a subsistence there. Once, in the winter, many years ago, when I had been cutting holes through the ice in order to catch pickerel, as I stepped ashore I tossed my axe back on to the ice, but, as if some evil genius had directed it, it slid four or five rods directly into one of the holes, where the water was twenty-five feet deep. Out of curiosity, I lay down on the ice and looked through the hole, until I saw the axe a little on one side, standing on its head, with its helve erect and gently swaying to and fro with the pulse of the pond; and there it might have stood erect and swaying till in the course of time the handle rotted off, if I had not disturbed it. Making another hole directly over it with an ice chisel which I had, and cutting down the longest birch which I could find in the neighborhood with my knife, I made a slip-noose, which I attached to its end, and, letting it down carefully, passed it over the knob of the handle, and drew it by a line along the birch, and so pulled the axe out again.

The shore is composed of a belt of smooth rounded white stones like paving-stones, excepting one or two short sand beaches, and is so steep that in many places a single leap will carry you into water over your head; and were it not for its remarkable transparency, that would be the last to be seen of its bottom till it rose on the opposite side. Some think it is bottomless. It is nowhere muddy, and a casual observer would say that there were no weeds at all in it; and of noticeable plants, except in the little meadows recently overflowed, which do not properly belong to it, a closer scrutiny does not detect a flag nor a bulrush, nor even a lily, yellow or white, but only a few small heart-leaves and potamogetons, and perhaps a water-target or two; all which however a bather might not perceive; and these plants are clean and bright like the element they grow in. The stones extend a rod or two into the water, and then the bottom is pure sand, except in the deepest parts, where there is usually a little sediment, probably from the decay of the leaves which have been wafted on to it so many successive falls, and a bright green weed is brought up on anchors even in midwinter. . . .

There have been caught in Walden pickerel, one weighing seven pounds,—to say nothing of another which carried off a reel with great velocity, which the fisherman safely set down at eight pounds because he did not see him,—perch and pouts, some of each weighing over two pounds, shiners, chivins or roach *(Leuciscus pulchellus),* a very few breams, and a couple of eels, one weighing four pounds,—I am thus particular because the weight of a fish is commonly its only title to fame, and these are the only eels I have heard of here;—also, I have a faint recollection of a little fish some five inches long, with silvery sides and a greenish back, somewhat dace-like in its character, which I mention here chiefly to link my facts to fable. Nevertheless, this pond is not very fertile in fish. Its pickerel, though not abundant, are its chief boast. I have seen at one time lying on the ice pickerel of at least three different kinds: a long and shallow one, steel-colored, most like those caught in the river; with greenish reflections and remarkably deep, which is the most common here; and another, golden-colored, and shaped like the last, but peppered on the sides with small dark brown or black spots, intermixed with a few faint blood-red ones, very much like a trout. The specific name *reticulatus* would not apply to this; it should be *guttatus* rather. These are all very firm fish, and weigh more than their size promises. The shiners, pouts, and perch also, and indeed all the fishes which inhabit this pond, are much cleaner, handsomer, and firmer fleshed than those in the river and most other ponds, as the water is purer, and they can easily be distinguished from them. Probably many ichthyologists would make new varieties of some of them. There are also a clean race of frogs and tortoises, and a few muscles in it; muskrats and minks leave their traces about it, and occasionally a travelling mud-turtle visits it. Sometimes, when I pushed off my boat in the morning, I disturbed a great mud-turtle which had secreted himself under the boat in the night. Ducks and geese frequent it in the spring and fall, the white-bellied swallows (*Hirundo bicolor*) skim over it, and the peetweets (*Totanus macularius*) "teter" along its stony shores all summer. I have sometimes disturbed a fish-hawk sitting on a white-pine over the water; but I doubt if it is ever profaned by the wing of a gull, like Fair Haven. At most, it tolerates one annual loon. These are all the animals of consequence which frequent it now.

You may see from a boat, in calm weather, near the sandy eastern shore, where the water is eight or ten feet deep, and also in some other parts of the pond, some circular heaps half a dozen feet in diameter by a foot in height, consisting of small stones less than a hen's egg in size, where all around is bare sand. At first you wonder if the Indians could have formed them on the ice for any purpose, and so, when the ice melted, they sank to the bottom; but they are too regular and some of them plainly too fresh for that. They are similar to those found pond westward you are obliged to employ both your hands to defend your eyes against the reflected as well as the true sun, for they are equally bright; and if, between the two, you survey its surface critically, it is literally as smooth as glass, except where the skater insects, at equal intervals scattered over its whole extent, by their motions in the sun produce the finest imaginable sparkle on it, or, perchance, a duck plumes itself, or, as I have said, a swallow skims so low as to touch it. It may be that in the distance a fish describes an arc of three or four feet in the air, and there is one bright flash where it emerges, and another where it strikes the water; sometimes the whole silvery arc is revealed; or here and there, perhaps, is a thistle-down floating on its surface, which the fishes dart at and so dimple it again. It is like molten glass cooled but not congealed, and the few motes in it are pure and beautiful like the imperfections in glass. You may often detect a yet smoother and darker water, separated from the rest as if by an invisible cobweb, boom of the water nymphs, resting on it. From a hill-top you can see a fish leap in almost any part; for not a pickerel or shiner picks an insect from this smooth surface but it manifestly disturbs the equilibrium of the whole lake. It is wonderful with what elaborateness this simple fact is advertised,—this piscine murder will out,—and from my distant perch I distinguish the circling undulations when they are half a dozen rods in diameter. You can even detect a water-bug (Gyrinus) ceaselessly progressing over the smooth surface a quarter of a mile off; for they furrow the water slightly, making a conspicuous ripple bounded by two diverging lines, but the skaters glide over it without rippling it perceptibly. When the surface is considerably agitated there are no skaters nor water-bugs on it, but apparently, in calm days, they leave their havens and adventurously glide forth from the shore by short impulses till they completely cover it. It is a soothing employment, on one of these fine days in the fall when all the warmth of the sun is fully appreciated, to sit on a stump on such a height as this, overlooking the pond, and study the dimpling circles which are incessantly inscribed on its otherwise and in November, usually, in a calm day, there is absolutely nothing to ripple the surface. One November afternoon, in the calm at the end of a rain storm of several days' duration, when the sky was still completely overcast and the air was full of mist, I observed that the pond was remarkably smooth, so that it was difficult to distinguish its surface; though it no longer reflected the bright tints of October, but the sombre November colors of the surrounding hills. Though I passed over it as gently as possible, the slight undulations produced by my boat extended almost as far as I could see, and gave a ribbed appearance to the reflections. But, as I was looking over the surface, I saw here and there at a distance a faint glimmer, as if some skater insects which had escaped the frosts might be collected there, or, per-chance, the surface, being so smooth, betrayed where a spring welled up from the bottom. Paddling gently to one of these places, I was surprised to find myself surrounded by myriads of small perch, about five inches long, of a rich bronze color in the green water, sporting there, and constantly rising to the surface and dimpling it, sometimes leaving bubbles on it. In such transparent and seemingly bottomless water, reflecting the clouds, I seemed to be floating through the air as in a balloon and their swimming impressed me as a kind of flight or hov-ering, as if they were a compact flock of birds passing just be-neath my level on the right or left, their fins, like sails, set all around them. There were many such schools in the pond, ap-parently improving the short season before winter would draw an icy shutter over their broad skylight, sometimes giving to the surface an appearance as if a slight breeze struck it, or a few rain-drops fell there. When I approached carelessly and alarmed them, they made a sudden plash and rippling with their rails, as if one had struck the water with a brushy bough, and in-stantly took refuge in the depths. At length the wind rose, the mist increased, and the waves began to run, and the perch leaped much higher than before, half out of the water, a hun-dred black points, three inches long, at once above the surface. Even as late as the firth of December, one year, I saw some dimples on the surface, and thinking it was going to rain hard immediately, the air being full of mist, I made haste to take my place at the oars and row homeward; already the rain seemed rapidly increasing, though I felt none on my cheek, and I anticipated a thorough soaking. But suddenly the dimples ceased, for they were produced by the perch, which the noise of my oars had scared into the depths, and I saw their schools dimly disappearing; so I spent a dry afternoon after all.

An old man who used to frequent this pond nearly sixty years ago, when it was dark with surrounding forests, tells me that in those days he sometimes saw it all alive with ducks and other water fowl, and that there were many eagles about it. He came here a-fishing, and used an old log canoe which he found on the shore. It was made of two white-pine logs dug out and pinned together, and was cut off square at the ends. It was very clumsy, but lasted a great many years before it became water-logged and perhaps sank to the bottom. He did not know whose it was; it belonged to the pond. He used to make a cable for his anchor of strips of hickory bark tied together. An old man, a potter, who lived by the pond before the Revolution, told him once that there was an iron chest at the bottom, and that he had seen it. Sometimes it would come floating up to the shore; but when you went toward it, it would go back into deep water and disappear. I was pleased to hear of the old log canoe, which took the place of an Indian one of the same material but more graceful construction, which perchance had first been a tree on the bank, and then, as it were, fell into the water, to float there for a generation, the most proper vessel for the lake. I remember that when I first looked into these depths there were many large trunks to be seen indistinctly lying on the bottom, which had either been blown over formerly, or left on the ice at the last cutting, when wood was cheaper; but now they have mostly disappeared.

When I first paddled a boat on Walden, it was completely surrounded by thick and lofty pine and oak woods, and in some of its coves grapevines had run over the trees next the water and formed bowers under which a boat could pass. The hills which form its shores are so steep, and the woods on them were then so high, that, as you looked down from the west end, it had the appearance of an amphitheatre for some kind of sylvan spectacle. I have spent many an hour, when I was younger, floating over its surface as the zephyr willed, having paddled my boat to the middle, and lying on my back across the seats, in a summer forenoon, dreaming awake, until I was aroused by the boat touching the sand, and I arose to see what shore my fates had impelled me to; days when idleness was the most attractive and productive industry. Many a forenoon have I stolen away, preferring to spend thus the most valued part of the day; for I was rich, if not in money, in sunny hours and summer days, and spent them lavishly; nor do I regret that I did not waste more of them in the workshop or the teacher's desk. But since I left those shores the woodchoppers have still further laid them waste, and now for many a year them will be no more rambling through the aisles of the wood, with occasional vistas through which you see the water. My Muse may be excused if she is silent henceforth. How can you expect the birds to sing when their groves are cut down?

Now the trunks of trees on the bottom, and the old log canoe, and the dark surrounding woods, are gone, and the villagers, who scarcely know where it lies, instead of going to the pond to bathe or drink, are thinking to bring its water, which should be as sacred as the Ganges at least, to the village in a pipe, to wash their dishes with!—to earn their Walden by the turning of a cock or drawing of a plug! That devilish Iron Horse, whose ear-rending neigh is heard throughout the town, has muddied the Boiling Spring with his foot, and he it is that has browsed off all the woods on Walden shore, that Trojan horse, with a thousand men in his belly, introduced by mercenary Greeks! Where is the country's champion, the Moore of Moore Hall, to meet him at the Deep Cut and thrust an avenging lance between the ribs of the bloated pest?

Nevertheless, of all the characters I have known, perhaps Walden wears best, and best preserves its purity. Many men have been likened to it, but few deserve that honor. Though the woodchoppers have laid bare first this shore and then that, and the Irish have built their sties by it, and the railroad has in-fringed on its border, and the ice-men have skimmed it once, it is itself unchanged, the same water which my youthful eyes fell on; all the change is in me. It has not acquired one perma-nent wrinkle after all its ripples. It is perennially young, and I may stand and see a swallow dip apparently to pick an insect from its surface as of yore. It struck me again to-night, as if I had not seen it almost daily for more than twenty years,— Why, here is Walden, the same woodland lake that I discovered so many years ago; where a forest was cut down last winter an-other is springing up by its shore as lustily as ever; the same thought is welling up to its surface that was then; it is the same liquid joy and happines to itself and its Maker, ay, and it *may* be to me. It is the work of a brave man surely, in whom there was no guile! He rounded this water with his hand, deepened and clarified it in his thought, and in his will bequeathed it to Concord. I see by its face that it is visited by the same reflec-tion; and I can almost say, Walden, is it you?

It is no dream of mine,
To ornament a line;
I cannot come nearer to God and Heaven
Than I live to Walden even.
I am its stony shore,
And the breeze that passes o'er;
In the hollow of my hand
Are its water and its sand
And its deepest resort
Lies high in my thought.

The cars never pause to look at it; yet I fancy that the engi-neers and firemen and brakemen, and those passengers who have a season ticket and see it often, are better men for the sight. The engineer does not forget at night, or his nature does not, that he has beheld this vision of serenity and purity once at least during the day. Though seen but once, it helps to wash out State-street and the engine's soot. One proposes that it be called "God's Drop."

The Education of a Forester

GIFFORD PINCHOT

Born into a family of lumber merchants, Gifford Pinchot, the founder of the U.S. Forest Service grew up with a distaste for the deforestation that wasted both human and natural resources. He also saw the waste that occurred when forests burned to the ground or were harvested without replanting. On the suggestion of his father, Pinchot decided to become a forester. But since no such profession existed in the United States in the 1880s, he decided to travel to France and study forestry with German forester Dietrich Brandis. The following selection shows how Pinchot began his education.

"Forestry," I wrote home, in the somewhat florid style of my age, "promises about all that my fondest dreams had hoped in the way of pleasant work, and I become more and mare convinced of the imperative need of Government control [of cutting] in the United States"—a conviction which has grown steadily with the years and was never so strong as now.

My head, of course, was full of questions. How soon could I learn what a competent forester must know? And where and how was I going to use what I was learning after I had learned it? Could I get a job in the Adirondacks, where the New York State Forest Preserve had been established, or in the South? And what were the conditions I would meet in the field?

My country was to me practically an unknown land. Fortunately I realized it. "I see more and more how foolish I have been not to get more fully acquainted with the facts at home when I had the chance. The whole question of a Forest Administration must turn on a thorough knowledge not only of

Excerpted from *Breaking New Ground*, by Gifford Pinchot (New York: Harcourt Brace, 1947). Reprinted with permission.

the forests but also of the laws and the people, and I am without either." Which was horse sense. And I went on to ask for a copy of *The American Citizen's Manual*.

I had never been West even so far as Niagara, which every living soul I met in Europe had heard of and wanted to know about. They all inquired whether I had seen it and what it was like; and every time I admitted I never had and didn't know, I lost caste visibly. One of the very first things I did when I got home was to go and see that majestic falling flood. I didn't propose to be caught that way again.

Like most exiles, the longer I was away from America the higher grew my pride in the Land of the Free, and the more interest I took in American affairs. As a citizen, I read the *Weekly Tribune* and the *Nation,* which was then the weekly New *York Evening post.* They took opposite sides on nearly every question and often left me guessing. As a forester, I studied *Garden and Forest* and the *Mississippi Valley Lumberman,* and those two differed no less than the others. I was learning, but the road was by no means easy.

For the Christmas holidays of 1889–90 I joined my old friend, James B. Reynolds, Yale '84, in Paris. On Christmas Day we two and nine other Americans played a team of French boys a very one-sided game of football in the Bois de Boulogne. On our side was the tradition of Yale Elevens which had been scored on only once in my four years. We ate them up.

From Paris I went again to see Dr. [Dietrich] Brandis in Bonn. He was convinced that "Nothing general can be done until some State or large individual owner makes the experiment and proves for America what is so well established in Europe, that forest management will pay." On this point Boppe and Brandis were agreed. No wonder their opinion was my lodestar for many years. . . .

A courteous and even ceremonious gentleman of the old school, yet practical as a pickax, Dr. Brandis never forgot that he was a scientist as well as an administrator—not always, in the hurly-burly of public life, an easy thing to do. In his declining years he turned again to botany, the love of his youth.

But he never ceased to be a forester, and never lost his interest in spreading his gospel in other lands.

Dr. Brandis' interest in Forestry did not stop with the forest. Forestry he regarded simply as one means to the general good. It was his chief concern, but he was hardly less devoted to political and social problems. His breadth of sympathy was remarkable. He was, for example, a vigorous champion of Christian missions, and in particular of American missionaries in Burma, where he had seen them at work; he was widely known in German labor circles; he had founded a workingmen's club in Bonn; and for years he gave one night a week to it.

To Dr. Brandis I owe more than I can ever tell. I doubt whether any other man in Europe could have been as wise a guide. Moreover, he could scarcely have taken more trouble with me if I had been his own son. As I look back, I think he saw in this long-legged youngster a possible instrument for bringing Forestry to a new continent.

At Nancy I wrote to him continually, and he to me. After I came home I sent him news and many questions about what was doing and needed to be done in American Forestry, and I never went abroad without going to see him. So long as he lived we never lost touch.

As I think it all over, I believe the greatest service Dr. Brandis did for me, and for the rest of his American students, was to inspire in us the same profound respect for Forestry as a profession that he held himself. Without that, groping in the murk of American public indifference, we would have been lost indeed.

The systems of forest management introduced in India by Dr. Brandis were, curiously enough, rather French than German. Admirable as German Forestry certainly was, there was about it too much artificial finish, too much striving for detailed perfection, too much danger that executive aggressiveness would be trained away, to fit it for use where Forestry was young.

Dr. Brandis never let his pupils forget a great truth which most German foresters had never grasped—that in the long run Forestry cannot succeed unless the people who live in and near the forest are for it and not against it. That was the keynote of his work in India. And when the pinch came, the application of that same truth was what saved the National Forests in America.

All in all, Brandis' services to American Forestry were so great that President Theodore Roosevelt sent him his photograph with this well-deserved inscription: "In high appreciation of the work of Sir Dietrich Brandis for the cause of forestry in the United States." I never saw a man more pleased with anything than Dr. Brandis was with that picture.

It was Dr. Brandis' yearly custom to take the English students from Cooper's Hill for a summer excursion through the most interesting forests of Germany and Switzerland. He was good enough to say I could join the tour when my work at Nancy was over.

It was a great chance, and I had to be ready to use it. What German I once knew had almost been forgotten. So I engaged a young medical student at Nancy to talk German with me when I walked for exercise. That brought my German back to a usable level.

Although retired and in his sixty-sixth year, Dr. Brandis still retained most of his famous energy and endurance. More than one British Indian forester has told me that on his inspection tours Brandis would walk down the forest officers of one district after another, leaving a train of worn-out men behind him. One down, t'other come on. He was one of the very few great trampers I have known that turned their toes out as they walked.

On my first day with the Cooper's Hill boys, Dr. Brandis' turned-out toes walked us through the forest for eight hours straight, without a bite to eat and without once sitting down, to the intense disgust of most of the English students. Their examinations had been passed, their positions in India were already secure. Why should they break their backs any further? But it seemed to me that we youngsters ought to be able to stand it if the Doctor could.

A number of these young Englishmen were very fine fellows indeed, and some were hard workers. For a few days, while Dr. Brandis was looking after one of them who had been taken sick, he asked me to step into his shoes. Said my diary: "Great sport being in command. Fellows are very nice, making no kick about anything." Which was less the rule than the exception.

My revived German often won me the chance to ride in the carriage (automobiles were still far below the horizon) with Dr. Brandis and the local forest officers, and listen to their expert discussions. All of these men were eager to tell about their own woodlands, and many of them were deeply interested in the American forest problem. It amounted almost to a liberal education.

At Dr. Brandis' suggestion, my Father had sent me a number of very large photographs of American forests. These pictures certainly paid their way. Wherever I showed them, as I did to every forester I could, they put me in position to hear discussions and learn facts that never would have been open to me without them.

In particular they got me the chance to talk with a number of the best foresters in Europe about what ought to be done in America. Most of these hard-working prints I gave away when the Brandis excursion was over, but one or two of them are with me yet. . . .

A month or two before sailing home, I wrote to my Father, asking him in substance what I was to do when I got back. How much of a gamble Forestry then was his answer made plain:

"It seems to me that you may fairly depend upon this, that in a very short time there will be something to do in this country for the man best prepared to decide upon Forestry matters. I cannot tell, but I feel all this, that the subject will soon have to be seriously considered and generally considered, and that you will have a chance somewhere. Don't fret about just how it is to come around."

The event proved him exactly right, but not to fret was easier said than done.

For my last bit of training Dr. Brandis sent me to stay with a Prussian Oberfoerster at Neupfalz, just back of Bingen-on-the-Rhine, and not so far from where our men crossed that great river shortly before Germany's surrender in 1945. There I put in a month studying the details of forest administration—the keeping of accounts and records, the making of reports, and so forth and so on. Fortunately I managed also to see something of forest management on the ground. Otherwise it was mainly time wasted, except for what I learned about the training of Prussian foresters and the Prussian point of view.

I shall never forget the old peasant who rose to his feet from his stone-breaking, as the Oberfoerster came striding along, and stood silent, head bent, cap in both hands, while that official stalked by without the slightest sign that he knew the peasant was on earth. And I remember also the shocked amazement of the whole family, male and female, when I declined to join in their Saturday night drinking bouts. Any way but their way was unthinkable.

In December the time I had allowed myself was up. I came home on a German freight boat which succeeded in making the passage in thirteen days and a half. We had head gales all the way. Even the paper on which I wrote a description of European forest policy, to be read at the annual meeting of the American Forestry Association, had to be held from sliding off the table. . . .

From the point of view of a fledgling forester, the situation when I got back left something to be desired. Unaware of the worst of it, I proceeded cheerfully to tackle the dragon Devastation in his own home cave.

Under the circumstances I had to play a lone hand. I could not join the denudatics, because they were marching up a blind alley. I could not join the lumbermen, because forest destruction was their daily bread. There was nothing left for me but to blaze my own trail.

The job was not to stop the ax, but to regulate its use. For that the whole stream of public thinking about the forest had to be shifted into a new channel—that of the few forest preservers no less than that of the many forest destroyers. A nation utterly absorbed in the present had to be brought to consider the future. The ingrained habit of mind of the best part of a hundred million people about a fundamental necessity of human life had to be changed.

I don't mean that I saw all this as clearly then as I do now. But at least I knew that I stood at the beginning of a long, long trail. It was probably just as well that I did not realize how rough and rocky that trail was going to be.

There were two possible ways of going at it. One was to urge, beg, and implore; to preach at, call upon, and beseech the American people to stop forest destruction and practice Forestry; and denounce them if they didn't. This was the method chosen by the Forestry Associations, by the Forestry Division, and by the friends of the forest generally.

This method got onto the platform and into the papers, but it never got into the woods. It had been followed for at least a quarter of a century, and still there was not a single case of systematic forest management in America to show for it.

The other plan was to put Forestry into actual practice in the woods, prove that it could be done by doing it, prove that it was practicable by making it work.

My good luck led me to choose action instead of exhortation. Indeed, I could hardly have done otherwise, for Dr. Brandis was never tired of urging me to prove the value of Forestry by practicing Forestry in the forest. The method of practical demonstration was literally "what the Doctor ordered."

Rich Land, Poor Land

STUART CHASE

Stuart Chase wrote the following selection in 1936 and linked the wealth of America with the abuse of the land. Like many conservationists of his generation, Stuart Chase used the idea of waste to persuade the public of the necessity of preservation. Here, Chase also introduces nostalgia for a lost virgin nature, a sense of gratitude to the bounty of nature, and a powerful aesthetic sense. Chase's work sounds very modern, in that almost all the concerns of the environmental movement are echoed in the selection.

How does the continent look today after three hundred years of occupation? Suppose we climb into a metaphorical airplane and cruise about America, first observing the whole picture, then circling to examine this area and that, finally looking into conditions underground—with the help of whatever scientific instruments may be necessary.

The basic map has changed but little: a slit across the Isthmus of Panama, a few minor shifts in the coast line, small islands thrown up here and there or washed away, some river channels recut. But coming closer we find the cover enormously changed, as well as the denizens thereof. The old forest, the old grasslands have almost completely disappeared. Desert lands have broadened. A dust desert is forming east of the Rockies where firm grass once stood. Woodlands—and a spindly lot they are by comparison—cover only half the area the primeval forest once covered. Grazing areas are still immense but the old types of native grasses have largely gone.

On one-quarter of continental United States are new fields,

Excerpted from *Rich Land, Poor Land*, by Stuart Chase (New York: McGraw-Hill, 1936).

bare in the winter, green with crops in the summer. Adjacent to these tilled fields are pasture lands, unknown before, of an almost equal area. On some of the old arid grasslands irrigation ditches now run, and between them is the green of crops. This is particularly noticeable around Salt Lake in Utah, in regions of the southwest, in the Imperial and Central valleys of California. Scattered about the continent, especially along the rivers and the sea coasts, are the black clusters of cities and the smaller dots of towns and villages. Linking them run a million miles and more of highways, railroads, the tracery of power lines, and pipe lines underground.

We drop 10,000 feet and look closer still. If this be progress, it is bitter tonic. The continental soil, the center of vitality, is visibly and rapidly declining. The forest cover has been stripped and burned and steadily shrinks. The natural grass cover has been torn to ribbons by steel plows and the hooves of cattle and sheep. The skin of America has been laid open. Streams have lost their measured balance, and, heavy with silt, run wild in flood to the sea at certain seasons, to fall to miserable trickles in the drier months. This land may be bristling with tall chimneys and other evidences of progress, but it has lost its old stability.

The humus is going, and when it is gone natural life goes. Two powerful agents are destroying the soil: erosion and the loss of fertility due to mining the soil for crops. Soils which have been building steadily for 20,000 years since the last ice age now in a single century lose the benefits of several thousand years of accumulation. Corn yields in sections of Iowa have dropped from 50 to 25 bushels per acre within the lifetime of a man not yet old. This, remember, is the richest soil in America.

One hundred million acres of formerly cultivated land has been essentially ruined by water erosion—an area equal to Illinois, Ohio, North Carolina and Maryland combined—the equivalent of 1,250,000 eighty-acre farms. In addition, this washing of sloping fields has stripped the greater part of the productive top soil from another 125 million acres now being cultivated. Erosion by wind and water is getting under way on another 100 million acres. More than 300 million acres—one-sixth of the country—is gone, going or beginning to go. This, we note, is on land originally the most fertile.

Kansas farms are blowing through Nebraska at an accelerating rate. In the spring of 1934, the farms of the Dust Bowl—which includes western Oklahoma, western Kansas, eastern Colorado, the panhandle of Texas and parts of Wyoming—blew clear out to the Atlantic Ocean, 2,000 miles away. On a single day 300 million tons of rich top soil was lifted from the Great Plains, never to return, and planted in places where it would spread the maximum of damage and discomfort. Authentic desert sand dunes were laid down. People began to die of dust pneumonia. More than nine million acres of good land has been virtually destroyed by wind erosion, and serious damage is reported on nearly 80 million acres.

Taking the continent as a whole, it is reliably estimated that half of its original fertility has been dissipated by these various agents. The rate of loss tends to follow the laws of compound interest. The stricken areas grow cumulatively larger.

From the packed earth of the crop lands, the bare-burned slopes of the devastated forests, the broken sods of the grasslands, rain and melting snow rush to the rivers in a fraction of the time they used to take. In some watersheds runoff which should require three months is carried down to the sea in a month. The rivers run red with mud where once they were clear. Reservoirs are filled, power dams rendered increasingly impotent. Lower a bucket into the Canadian River and allow it to settle. One-quarter of the water turns out to be rich soil which the upstream owner paid for in cash.

The baked earth of the tilled fields prevents the rain from percolating into the artesian basins as it used to percolate through the cover of forest and grass. We see the underground water table falling all over the western half of the continent. In the Dakotas and Iowa the drop is serious; in the Central Valley of California, it is still more serious. Meanwhile pumping for irrigation helps to exhaust the basins. The cool, dark reservoirs which once did so much to equalize flood and drought are sinking. The same is happening with surface reservoirs. Marshes and swamps have been drained in the hope of reclaiming good agricultural land. Sometimes the land is good and sometimes it is bad, unsuited for crops. When it is bad, fires course through the dried underbrush, as in the sterile Wisconsin and Minnesota marshes.

In the lower reaches of the rivers, the old natural side reservoirs have been blocked off by levees. Here is rich farm land, to be sure, but the rivers rise as the silt sinks, and the levees must rise higher still. In New Orleans at flood crests, the Mississippi runs high above the streets of the town. River channels are straightened and further aid the rush to the ocean. Levees break; indeed the whole levee system nears its breaking point as a practicable engineering method for flood control.

Floods under these conditions must grow worse; droughts must grow worse. The safeguards of nature have been stripped away. In times of low water, the pollution of streams becomes an ominous menace. Each community in the watershed area dumps its untreated sewage into the drinking supply of the town below. When the river is low, sewage poisons remain unoxidized.

In uncounted streams, fish lie killed by the wastes of cities and the black refuse of mine and factory. Pollution has destroyed more fish than all the fishermen, and silt has killed more than pollution. When the sun cannot get through because of the mud, the tiny water plants die and fish lose their basic food supply. Oil wastes strangle the fish fry when they come to the surface. Sewage competes with marine life for a limited oxygen supply. Waxy sludge coats the river bottoms and kills plants there. Our streams, according to [Paul] Sears, have become watery deserts, inimical to life. Simpletons try to restock them. "To release millions of fingerlings into such an environment and expect them to live is like driving a flock of yearlings into Death Valley."

The last passenger pigeon died in the Cincinnati Zoo in 1914, the sole survivor on earth of the "most abundant and the most beautiful of all American game birds." Toward the end, a single season's slaughter in Michigan accounted for five million of these creatures. The last heath hen died on Martha's Vineyard in 1932. Recently Mr. William Finley, naturalist and wild-life photographer, exhibited two films of the lower Klamath region in Oregon. The first was taken in 1915 and showed a great watershed swarming with game birds and migratory waterfowl. The second was taken twenty years later and showed the same area despoiled by promoters, a biological desert devoid of water, food or cover and forsaken by the birds which once lived and nested there. Birds, it must never be forgotten, are the chief enemies of insects. Without their protection plant life and animal life are thrown out of equilibrium, while life for man speedily becomes unendurable.

Besides the material and financial loss here represented, an environment lovely to the eye has been sacrificed. The most hideous spots are the environs of mines and the slums and industrial areas of great cities. Gashed earth, culm banks, dead trees and streams putrid with chemicals, refuse and coal dust distinguish the mines. Cities seem to pride themselves on turning their river banks or waterfronts into majestic privies. Here cluster smoking dumps high as Bunker Hill, gas works, sewer outlets, dilapidated coal sheds, switch yards, oil refineries, slaughterhouses, glue factories, tanneries which stun the nose and great barges laden down with garbage. Yet these waters determined the location of the city in the first place, and have often been its chief builder and nourisher. Can ingratitude go farther? European cities respect their waters and adorn their banks with parks, boulevards and public buildings. Latin-American countries do the same. Compare the waterfront of Havana with that of Brooklyn or Hoboken.

In place of green foliage and clear water, man has brought to the continent of America stinking rivers, charred forests, the incomparable filth of cities, the wretched shacks of tenant farmers along Tobacco Road.

Suppose present trends were to be projected unaltered into the future. I have had an opportunity to look at that future, not with a magical electric eye but with my own. In a certain area these trends have been speeded up with the aid of chemistry, and the future now stands stark for all to see. The normal processes of erosion are mechanical and take longer in the working out. But the end is substantially the same. The hills of the country I am about to describe are as terrible as the man-killed hills of China, but they have been blasted by the sulphuric acid fumes of a copper smelter rather than by the stripping of forest and grass.

We left Knoxville, Tennessee, in a March snow squall and headed south along a broad concrete highway. Presently the sun came out and revealed the Great Smoky Mountains really smoking like Popocatepetl. The road passed beside a muddy river, log cabins, rail fences, steep cornfields, some of them badly gullied. At the town of Benton we turned east, steering for a 4,000-foot pass in the mountains, close to the Georgia line. The road climbed steeply up the river valley and the mountainsides drew closer. Suddenly we came upon a large concrete dam and powerhouse, beside it a steam power plant and a tourist hotel, beset with notice boards. Behind the dam in the mountain gorge was a long narrow lake called the Ocoee reservoir, in which the water was very low. This, like the hotel, the powerhouse and the road belonged to a private power company—a big, costly development.

The scenery was wild and impressive: sheer precipices, deep ravines, tumbling cascades, the gray lake. Rocks lay on the road where they had fallen from cliffs above. It must require a considerable crew to clear this road of avalanches. We turn a bend and suddenly see a thing that belongs in no lake. It is a chocolate-colored tongue of shaking mud, half a mile long, and behind it are other tongues and trembling islands. These are deposits of silt, brought down by the water from the lands above. The formations are about six feet high, constantly caving in where the current strikes them. The whole upper end of the reservoir is full of them. The banks themselves have changed from good honest mud to this forbidding red-brown jelly.

We entered the narrow gorge with the river. There was

hardly room for both of us. It was a river not of water but of boiling molasses. The whole stream bed, every rock, every log, every leaf of grass, was coated with silt. We passed another power plant. Across the gorge a wooden flume ran for four or five miles along the mountainside, leaping the side ravines on steel bridges. It seemed to be bearing water from some higher level. The trees about us were dead. Great charred logs thrust hideously out of the perpendicular slopes of the gorge. Mile upon mile had been blasted by fire.

Up, up, we went. Suddenly the mountain wall to the east dissolved and we looked over a broad expanse of bare rounded hills faintly green. They looked like the hills near San Francisco and seemed strangely out of place in Tennessee. Beyond the fire area were live trees again, some in their first spring raiment. Another mile and they began to die. It was not fire this time, but something still more unnatural.

We were among the rounded hills. There were bunches of withered grass on them and the occasional white skeleton of a tree. They were ribbed with cracks through which the red earth appeared. In some places terracing had been attempted to hold the soil, but the terraces had long since been breached with raw open gullies. Fences fell crazily into these gulfs. The earth was opening about us; the road seemed the only firm place. Grass remained but it was functionless, its holding power gone. I cannot tell you what it means to see and feel the power of the earth cover gone. Anything might happen. Here was no place for life or for man. The gullies grew wider and deeper—twenty feet, thirty feet down, a hundred feet across. The hills burst open like a skinless dry peach. Then even the dead grass disappeared. The desolation was monstrous and complete, like mountains on the moon.

Over a crest we saw a cloud of black smoke. The road curved around the crest and Ducktown rose before us—a little village and a huge dark smelter perched on a hill. In a great circle about the smelter, measuring perhaps ten miles in diameter, every living thing had been destroyed by the sulphur fumes. These were badlands without the balance and natural composure of a desert. Here was a wall-sided red brick school-house with ten-foot gullies of livid earth leading up to it. Here a lone house with a tiny green garden, protected by heaven knows what labor and what chemistry against the sulphur. We pass a sign, WELCOME TO DUCKTOWN, and enter a huddle of wretched houses crouched under the bleak walls of the gigantic smelter, the land rushing away from every doorstep.

Inside the town, the horror is momentarily shut out. Main Street as usual—drugstore, cinema, Masonic hall, A & P, filling station, garages, motorcars parked at proper angles against the curb, people talking, shopping, smiling. COME AGAIN TO DUCKTOWN.

We halt the car at a lookout on the far side of the hill beyond the houses. Across a blasted plain on the northeast we see the far horizon with hills and trees again. Thank God for trees! We head the car for those far woodlands.

People live in Ducktown. Main Street bustles as in Middletown. Incredible. But on second thought it is the most appropriate setting for Main Street. Ugliness matches ugliness, and desolation suits desolation. A raw commercial age merits such a background, where nature throws up her hands and the good earth runs bleeding to the sea. Before it finds the ocean, it chokes the power company's reservoir. This, too, is as it should be. The true spirit of individualism. The copper company ruins the reservoir; the power company seeks whom it may devour farther down the stream.

Ducktown. The symbol of the logical end of an undirected machine age. It supports the gas stations, billboards, schoolhouses and Masonic lodges of Main Street out of the bowels of the earth with good red copper. But in the process the land has gone. Presently silt will completely fill the reservoir and no more electric power will come over the lines to Ducktown. The mine elevators will stop. Ducktown will perish. Its subterranean workers will perish. Its shacks and garages will slide into fifty-foot gullies. The belching sulphur fumes will cease. Life has gone and man must now go. The years pass. The grass begins to creep back on the edges of the desert ten miles away.

After the grass come pine seedlings and oak. They come slowly, for Nature has a great wound to heal. In a thousand years, perhaps, the humus will return, the streams will run clear, the great lateral cracks will be overgrown, the gullies will be filled, and earth creatures may live once more in Ducktown—where wild ducks lived before man came.

Here is the whole story of the future—"if present trends continue"—highly simplified and very clear. Metaphorically speaking, the smelter is industry, feeding on a declining resource. While that resource lasts, the people of Ducktown have jobs and automobiles. The world congratulates Ducktown on its high standard of living. Meanwhile the land crumbles away and the waters become wild and useless. This does not matter—for men without eyes—if other lands grow food and if copper keeps coming out of the mines to exchange for it. But no mine can be operated without power, and finally the outraged land and water cut off the power. What happens then? What happens when the copper runs out? What happens when other lands cease to grow crops, by virtue of Ducktowns of their own? What happens when a continent is one great Ducktown?

CHRONOLOGY

1607
The first permanent British settlement in North America, Jamestown, is established.

1785
The Land Ordinance Act is passed.

1827
The first volume of James Audubon's *The Birds of America* is published.

1830–1850
Rail network in the United States greatly expands, opening large tracts of wilderness to settlers.

1844
George Catlin's *North American Portfolio* is published.

1854
Thoreau's *Walden Pond* is published.

1862
The Homestead Act is passed by the U.S. Congress.

1865
George Perkins Marsh's *Man and Nature* is published.

1872
The first national park in the United States, Yellowstone, is established.

1892
John Muir founds the Sierra Club.

1905
The U.S. Forest Department is established under the leadership of Gifford Pinchot.

1909
Theodore Roosevelt urges Congress to create the National Conservation Commission.

1935
The Wilderness Society is founded.

1946
The federal government's Bureau of Land Management is established.

1949
A Sand County Almanac, authored by Aldo Leopold, is published.

1960
Congress passes the Clean Water Act.

1962
Silent Spring, authored by Rachel Carson, is published.

1963
Congress passes the Clean Air Act.

1964
Congress passes the Wilderness Act.

1965
Congress passes the Water Quality Act.

1968

The Population Bomb, authored by Paul Ehrlich, is published; Congress passes the Wild and Scenic Rivers Act and the National Trails System Act.

1969

President Richard M. Nixon signs the National Environmental Policy Act into law.

1970

Earth Day is first celebrated.

1973

Small Is Beautiful, authored by E.F. Schumacher, is published.

1974

President Nixon signs the Safe Drinking Water Act.

1980

President Ronald Reagan signs "Superfund" legislation mandating cleanup of toxic waste dumps.

1987

President Reagan signs the Montreal Protocol, an agreement to phase out production of ozone-depleting chemicals.

1992

The first Earth Summit is held in Rio de Janeiro, Brazil.

2001

The United States withdraws from the Kyoto Protocol, an international agreement to limit carbon dioxide emissions.

FOR FURTHER RESEARCH

Edward Abbey, *Desert Solitaire*. New York: Ballantine, 1998.

Paul Brooks, *Speaking for Nature: How Literary Naturalists from Henry Thoreau to Rachel Carson Have Shaped America*. San Francisco: Sierra Club Books, 1980.

Rachel Carson, *Silent Spring*. Boston: Houghton Mifflin, 1962.

Barry Commoner, *Making Peace with the Planet*. New York: Pantheon Books, 1990.

Robert C. Cook, *Human Fertility: The Modern Dilemma*. New York: W. Sloane Associates, 1951.

William Cronon, *Nature's Metropolis*. Cambridge, MA: Blackwell, 1994.

Mark Dowie, *Losing Ground: American Environmentalism at the Close of the Twentieth Century*. Cambridge, MA: MIT Press, 1995.

Riley E. Dunlap and Angela G. Mertig, eds., *American Environmentalism: The U.S. Environmental Movement, 1970–1990*. Philadelphia: Taylor & Francis, 1992.

Anne H. Ehrlich and Paul R. Ehrlich, *Earth*. New York: Franklin Watts, 1987.

Environmental Viewpoints: Selected Essays and Excerpts on Issues in Environmental Protection. 3 vols. Detroit: Gale Research, 1992–1994.

Osborn Fairfield, *Our Plundered Planet*. Boston: Little, Brown, 1948.

Ronald Foresta, *America's National Parks and Their Keepers*. Washington, DC: Resources for the Future, 1984.

Samuel Hays, *Beauty, Health, and Permanence: Environmental Politics in the United States 1955–1985.* New York: Cambridge University Press, 1987.

J. Douglas Hurt, *Indian Agriculture in America: Prehistory to the Present.* Lawrence: University Press of Kansas, 1987.

James Howard Kunstler, *The Geography of Nowhere: The Rise and Decline of America's Man-Made Landscape.* New York: Simon and Schuster, 1994.

Frank N. Magill, ed., *Great Events from history II.* Ecology and the Environment series. 5 vols. Pasadena, CA: Salem Press, 1995.

James Malin, *The Grassland of North America Prolegomena to Its History.* Gloucester, MA: P. Smith, 1947.

Bill McKibben, *The End of Nature.* New York: Random House, 1989.

Roderick Nash, ed., *American Environmentalism: Readings in Conservation History.* New York: McGraw-Hill, 1990.

David Orr, *Ecological Literacy: Education and the Transition to a Postmodern World.* Albany: State University of New York Press, 1992.

Harold Steen, *The U.S. Forest Service: A History.* Seattle: University of Washington Press, 1976.

Douglas H. Strong, *Dreamers and Defenders: American Conservationists.* Lincoln: University of Nebraska Press, 1988.

Michael Williams, *Americans and Their Forests: A Historical Geography.* New York: Cambridge University Press, 1989.

Anthony B. Wolbarst, ed., *Environment in Peril.* Washington, DC: Smithsonian Institution Press, 1991.

Donald Worster, *Nature's Economy: A History of Ecological Ideas.* New York: Cambridge University Press, 1995.

INDEX

activism
  political, 157
  radical, can help protect
    environment, 156–64
Alaska, 106
Americans and Their Forests: A
  Historical Geography
  (Michael Williams), 35
ancient societies
  earth worship among,
    60–63
Anderson, Sherwood, 122
Atlantic Monthly (magazine),
  102
Aune, Phil, 134
Austin, Mary, 127

Berman, Morris, 64
Bessey, Charles, 73
Brandis, Dietrich, 193
Breaking New Ground
  (Pinchot), 192
Bryant, William Cullen, 40
Bush, George H.W., 165

Carson, Rachel, 18
Catlin, George, 172
Changes in the Land: Indians,
  Colonists, and the Ecology of
  New England (Cronon), 22
Chase, Stuart, 199
Chateaubriand, 39
Christian tradition
  Four Cardinal Virtues of,
    149–50

Circular No. 21, 94, 99
civil disobedience, 160–61
Clark-McNary Act (1924),
  98
Clean Air Act, 18
Clements, Frederick, 17, 72,
  73, 75
Cleveland, Grover, 16
climax community. *See* Great
  Plains
Cline, McGarvey, 99
Clothier, George L., 97
coal, 86
  depletion of, 88
Cole, Thomas, 40
colonists, American
  changes in views of forests,
    35–44
  vs. Native Americans, in
    interaction with nature, 29
  observations on Native
    American practices by,
    23–24
conifers
  success of, 130–32
conservation
  expansion of federal role in,
    92–100
conservation movement
  diminution of forests and,
    14–15
  vs. environmental
    movement, 16
Cooper, James Fenimore, 40
Cooper, William, 37

Greenpeace, 160
Gross National Product
  (GNP)
  increases in, and destruction
    of nature, 152

Herbert, George, 53
Hetch Hetchy Valley, 16
Higginson, Francis, 28
history, U.S.
  agrarian ideal in, 38–39
  ecological interpretation of,
    117–18
  role of natural resource
    discovery in, 86
Hooke, Robert, 67
Hooker, Joseph, 111
Hough, Franklin, 14
human(s)
  are inextricably linked to
    nature, 45–58
  changes to natural world by,
    104
  destructiveness of, 77–80
  vs. animals, 80–82
  duty of, to posterity, 89–90
  Earth's long-term carrying
    capacity of, 137, 140–41
  etymology of, 62
  land ethic changes in role
    of, 116
  must lead ecologically
    responsible lives, 151–55
  population, growth in, 137,
    166
    fertility/mortality rates
      and, 138
  should emulate ancient
    attitudes toward nature,
    59–68

total impact on Earth's
  ecosystems, 143–44
as wild species, 121

"Intelligent Husbandry"
  (Madison), 30
Interior Department, U.S.
  cooperation with Bureau of
    Forestry, 96–98
Irving, Washington, 39, 40

Jackson, Andrew, 37
Jefferson, Thomas, 38

King, Martin Luther, Jr., 161
King Philip's Uprising, 36

land
  need for "improvement" of,
    37–39
  ownership of, and intensity
    of use, 13
  supply of, and labor
    expense, 30–32
land ethic, 116
Lechford, Thomas, 27
Legend of Sleepy Hollow, The
  (Irving), 39
Leopold, Aldo, 71, 114
Levett, Christopher, 27
Lilienthal, David, 71
literature
  effects of urbanization on,
    122–23
  of romantic movement,
    39–41
  rural ideal in, 39
Locke, John, 13
Lovejoy, Sam, 161